HEADHUNTERS
CONFIDENTIAL

HEADHUNTERS CONFIDENTIAL

125 Insider Secrets
to Landing Your Dream Job

ALAN R. SCHONBERG

Chairman of the World's Largest Executive Recruiting Firm

Management Recruiters International, Inc.

with
Robert L. Shook

McGRAW-HILL

New York   San Francisco   Washington, D.C.   Auckland   Bogotá
Caracas   Lisbon   London   Madrid   Mexico City   Milan   Montreal
New Delhi   San Juan   Singapore   Sydney   Tokyo   Toronto

McGraw-Hill

A Division of The McGraw·Hill Companies

1 2 3 4 5 6 7 8 9 0   DOC/DOC   0 9 8 7 6 5 4 3 2 1 0

ISBN 0-07-136189-8
ISBN 0-07-135230-9 (pbk)

This publication is designed to provide accurate and authoritative information in regard to the subject matter covered. It is sold with the understanding that the publisher is not engaged in rendering legal, accounting, or other professional service. If legal advice or other expert assistance is required, the services of a competent professional person should be sought.

> —*From a declaration of principles jointly adopted by a committee*
> *of the American Bar Association and a committee of publishers.*

This book is printed on recycled, acid-free paper containing a minimum of 50% recycled de-inked fiber.

McGraw-Hill books are available at special quantity discounts to use as premiums and sales promotions, or for use in corporate training programs. For more information, please write to the Director of Special Sales, Professional Publishing, McGraw-Hill, 2 Penn Plaza, New York, NY 10121. Or contact your local bookstore.

This book is dedicated to my wife,
Carole, our children, and our grandchildren.
It is also dedicated to my extended MRI family,
without whom this book could not have been written.

Contents

SECTION II. THE INTERVIEW

SECTION III. THE POSTINTERVIEW

Acknowledgments

My special thanks goes to the wonderful MRI professionals who shared their expertise with me. Their contributions were invaluable.

Vince Webb, the company's dynamic marketing vice president, and his director of field-office marketing, Karen Bloomfield, worked with me from the beginning to the completion of the entire manuscript. They participated in the initial stages when the book was just an idea, and they served as a liaison with my coauthor, Bob Shook, throughout the entire writing process. Their creative contributions and inspiration are very much appreciated, as was the capable help of their administrative assistant, Michelle Franz.

Special thanks to literary agent Al Zuckerman, president of Writers House, who's the best in his field. Kudos also to senior editor Betsy Brown at McGraw-Hill, who also is a star in her own right, and to Pattie Amoroso, our outstanding editing supervisor. And many thanks to two talented people, Stormy Bailey and Frank Lesser, who spent many hours assisting in transcribing, typing, and editing, and then retyping and reediting.

Last but not least, it's been a pleasure to collaborate on a book a second time with Bob Shook. I admire his dedication, discipline, and professionalism, and most of all, his friendship.

Introduction

C hanging jobs is one of life's most stressful experiences—even if it's an upward move. This should come as no surprise. Most of us resist change of any kind. And a dramatic career shift affects all aspects of our lives. In addition to work-satisfaction aspects and financial matters, it spills over into our personal lives, so our spouses and children also feel the effects. Being pressured and unsettled at the office can even affect our health.

It doesn't matter how good your résumé reads or how strong the economy is, a job search is a difficult, time-intensive task. This is true even when there are low unemployment and labor shortages. During boom times, an average job search takes three months.

Having spent the last 36 years in the executive search industry, I am writing this book for anyone going through—or thinking about—a job change. My message benefits anyone who is (1) in between jobs, (2) seriously considering a change due to job-related frustration, or (3) simply interested in some career management ideas. If you fall into this third category and are content with your present job, I recommend you still touch base with headhunters so you can stay current with your industry. In particular, this will apprise you of what other people with similar jobs are earning.

I am also writing this book because most of the books and articles I've read on changing jobs are filled with misinformation. This is particularly true when it comes to the interview process—which my colleagues and I believe is the most crucial factor in getting a job offer. Hear me out, and you'll be privy to expert advice from scores of the best in the headhunting business.

Because knowing how to interview effectively is vital, I have organized this book into three sections, centering on the job interview:

Section I. The Preinterview, Section II. The Interview, and Section III. The Postinterview.

Remember, there are only a handful of occasions in your life when you actually search for a job. It's an area in which you have, at best, little experience. Compared to the quantity of time you'll likely work during your lifetime (about 90,000 hours), it is, indeed, an infinitesimal amount. Yet studies reveal that people who excel at the job-search process will enjoy substantially higher earnings over the course of their careers. In other words, those relatively few hours put into the job search can produce hundreds of thousands of extra paycheck dollars. It behooves you to do a good job in your search for a job!

THE PREINTERVIEW

When the subject of changing jobs comes up, most people become uncomfortable thinking about an eyeball-to-eyeball encounter with a recruiter. MRI studies substantiate that the interview process is a major determinant on whether a job offer is made. Simply put, it makes good sense to be properly prepared for your interviews. In this section, you'll learn how to assure a successful interview. You'll also find out how being unprepared guarantees your interview will bomb.

1

Take a Self-Inventory

If you had a business to sell, you'd probably inventory your assets before putting it on the market. The same thing applies to putting yourself on the market. Here, too, you must determine what you have to sell—and how much you are worth to a prospective employer.

Granted, this is no easy task. Just the same, you must identify and evaluate your specific talents. Perhaps the best way to accomplish this is by isolating yourself. Find a quiet room, an out-of-the-way spot in the country or on a remote beach where you can be alone—and think! Think about what you have done in the past that will enable you to succeed in the future. Your talents and experiences have equipped you with particular skills that some particular company needs. Although your assets are intangible, they have a definite value. It's essential that you identify these before you talk to a headhunter or prospective employer. You must also know your liabilities. Your liabilities will be specific shortcomings that may hamper your success in a particular position. For instance, certain computer skills are essential in today's business world. Candidates who are strong in this area may leave you in the dust. Likewise, not having an MBA degree might put you behind candidates who attended graduate school.

The more experience you have, the better the chance prospective employers will assess you without regard to where you went to college or how many diplomas you accumulated. So when taking a self-inventory, consider everything you have done that qualifies you for the position you seek, including the contributions you made to your previous employers. Job performance reveals what you are capable of contributing in the future.

In summary, your history and your potential worth to another company tells a prospective employer what to pay for services he or she believes you can provide. Unfortunately, many qualified job candidates take an inadequate self-inventory and, consequently, have no idea of their potential worth. It's a shame because these otherwise qualified candidates get passed over—and somebody else gets the job that should have been theirs!

One last tip for those of you who think you're on top of it: today's prize-winning horse may be tomorrow's slow-drying glue. Time has a way of passing rather quickly, so every two to three years, you're due for another inventory. To stay current, you must look at yourself to know what you have to offer the current job market. In my opinion, this is mandatory for prudent career management.

2

Put It in Writing

More often than not, qualified job candidates assess themselves poorly. As a consequence, they are clueless about what they have to offer prospective employers. Some underestimate their real worth while others overestimate it. Such flawed judgment is potentially harmful. It's essential to understand who you are and accurately communicate this to recruiters.

My best advice: *put it in writing*. If you don't, it's likely that you'll be vague about what you have to offer and have difficulty articulating it. Oftentimes, people refuse to accept themselves as they truly are. They have abandoned their youthful dreams, but they refuse to acknowledge it. Deluding yourself is no way to land a dream job. You must be realistic. This is why taking a self-inventory in black and white is imperative. It allows you to analyze clearly your strengths and your weaknesses. By putting it on paper, you'll have a clear, concise outline of who you are, something tangible that you can see and frequently review. Left in your head, it's nothing more than an abstract opinion, one that's apt to be slightly inflated!

I also recommend keeping a journal of your short-term and long-term career goals. Charting out where you want to be in the near and distant future keeps you on target. It also gives you direction. Periodic reviews of your journal let you know if you're on or off course. This enables you to adjust or even change courses. Without having concise goals on paper, people have a tendency to drift. It's like taking a cross-country trip without a map. You may think you know where you are going, but the likelihood of getting lost is substantially greater. Don't get lost on your career path—the stakes are too high.

3

What If the Money Didn't Matter?

With a mortgage, car payments, and credit cards, I know that money *does* matter. I also know that today's working parents need a lot of money to raise and educate young children. Welcome to the real world.

But think back to when your dreams were fresh. Remember thinking about having a career you could truly enjoy—or perhaps one in which you could make a difference in the world? For most people, things didn't turn out the way they expected, and they've long since settled for something less than a dream job. They made a lot of compromises along the way and ended up doing things they swore they'd never do. Some people accept this and chalk it up to maturity. "I wasn't being realistic," they claim. Or, they say, "I have responsibilities, so I'm obligated to make certain sacrifices. I can't afford to do the kind of work I'd enjoy."

Horsefeathers! They are copping out, and I don't buy it. They had wonderful dreams, but for one reason or another they gave up on them. Perhaps certain obstacles discouraged them, and they lost confidence. Or people told them that it couldn't be done, and they believed them. Then, too, maybe they met failure along the way, and it defeated them. They simply lost the will to push forward because it was too difficult.

If you're at a turning point, seeking a career change, think back to those early dreams you abandoned along the way. Keep them in mind when making your future plans. Maybe you'll have to choose between two jobs—one that pays well and one that would give you more satisfaction and enjoyment. Ask yourself, "What if the money didn't matter?"

The truth is, you should never give up on your dreams. Even if you can't afford to pursue them, you mustn't quit. I have found that the most successful people are those who love what they do—and they'd do it for less money rather than do something else. Their love for their work is apparent. This increases their energy level and makes them superior to others who simply go through the motions. These lucky people look forward to coming to work every day. They're not driven by the size of their paychecks, but their superior everyday performance greatly enhances their annual earnings.

By taking a lower paying job which inspires and rewards you, you may be more productive, which may yield bigger paychecks down the road. So, even though the money doesn't matter, you're still going to get it!

In summary, the desire to make more money should never be your primary motivation in a job search. Go for the job that excites you and offers the best long-term opportunities.

At MRI, the leading job candidates we've studied say that money ranks seventh in their reasons for seeking a new job. These six things are more important than getting more money:

1. Having more opportunity

2. Being part of a dynamic company, being accepted

3. Being involved in making decisions

4. Being challenged

5. Being responsible for specific tasks or duties

6. Being recognized for doing a good job

4

What Do You Want to Do for the Rest of Your Life?

This is a difficult question for most people. Depending on where they are in their careers, the answer can elude them. For young people in the early stages of their careers, it's sometimes impossible to know. Only with adequate experience can they accurately address this question. Often they must go through one or more jobs before they recognize what opportunities exist. In my early 20s, I didn't have the foggiest notion that I'd someday be the head of a search company. The truth is, back then I didn't even know what a headhunter was!

It takes some time to get a feel for business—what you'll feel comfortable doing, and, for that matter, what you'll dislike. With exposure and effective networking, doors will open that you never knew existed early in your career.

Further on in your career, you should have a clearer goal about what to do for the rest of your life. If you don't, you must do some serious soul searching. Without a clear goal, you can drift for years—and reach an age where the pickings are slim. I pity the poor soul who drifts from job to job, never finding a niche. Such people live frustrated lives.

Remember that it's okay to know what you want to do for the rest of your life, and later change your mind. It's natural to change your mind: as circumstances change, so do long-term goals. Always keep in mind that everything in this world is subject to change, including lifetime ambitions.

5

What Can You Uniquely Offer an Employer?

C hances are high you're competing with several people for the same job. In fact, the number of qualified candidates can range from 2 to 20. If several headhunters are involved, you can assume all the candidates are qualified.

With a wide array of candidates, the job will likely go to the person who stands apart from the herd. This person has addressed the question, "How am I unique to this employer?"

Granted, résumés are like fingerprints—each is unique. But while your résumé may get you through the door, it alone won't set you apart from the others. If you're working with a headhunter, ask, "What is the most important thing this company wants in a candidate?" This advance information gives you a decisive edge. It enables you to come to the interview with a summary of your qualifications based precisely on what the employer is seeking.

If you cannot get this information, assess your career to identify your greatest accomplishment. Ask yourself, "What have I done that makes me most proud?" Once you can answer this question, you will know what you can uniquely offer an employer.

In a highly competitive job search involving many candidates, the recruiter may conduct a series of interviews over an extended period of time. Remembering who's who becomes difficult. It's not unusual for a recruiter to forget what one candidate looks like, let alone what was said over the course of several days. If the recruiter can't remember who you are, how do you expect to rise above the other candidates?

Some candidates employ gimmicks, ranging from wearing a boutonniere to telling an outrageous story. I remember one candidate who performed sleight-of-hand magic tricks so he'd be remembered!

Please, no gimmicks. The higher up the corporate ladder you're looking, the more this applies. Senior management positions require individuals who can assume a lot of responsibility. This is not a time for frivolity. Attract notice because you're sharp, perceptive, attentive, and well prepared.

I am personally attracted to the candidate who shows a passion for work. When you truly love what you do, this comes through crystal clear to everyone. And remember: nothing is as contagious as enthusiasm.

6

A Journal of Your Accomplishments

I recommend that everyone keep a journal—not just people in search of their dream jobs. It's never too soon—or too late—to start listing your accomplishments. You don't need an elaborate journal. A large notebook with dividers works fine. Write down your important achievements on a regular basis, say, weekly. In the beginning, this may seem difficult or even silly. In any event, write down the single biggest accomplishment of the week, even if it's just being invited to lunch by your boss. As time goes by, you'll accumulate a lot of entries.

Documenting your achievements serves many purposes. For starters, it's good exercise for tracking your career. With your achievements on paper, you can review your progress, or, for that matter, see where you've stalled. The impatient can see they are advancing, even if the pace seems slow at times. A journal can highlight areas for your improvement. In short, it's a way of having your own scorecard. You can track your hits, runs, and errors, and see where you need coaching.

You never know when a record of important dates and events might come in handy. You might need to put together a quick résumé to take advantage of a rare opportunity. A well-written journal can save you hours of gathering the right places and times—everything is right at your fingertips when you need it.

When appropriate, a journal of your accomplishments is also an impressive tool in an interview. An architect, for example, might use a journal to illustrate step-by-step progress on a particular project. This log of concept and execution, with accompanying obstacles and how they were overcome, exhibits job skills vital to any employer. This is an excellent proactive technique—a subject I will address later on.

Finally, reviewing your journal is a great way to "pump up" just before a job interview. You'll remember all sorts of past achievements long forgotten—things you'll find appropriate to discuss with the interviewer. As one successful job candidate told me, "Reflecting on my past successes reinforced who I am. What a great way to boost one's self-confidence."

7

A Lifetime
Self-Improvement Program

In the world of business, you either go forward or backward—there's no such thing as sitting still. I'm reminded of the advice the Red Queen gave Alice in *Through the Looking-Glass*. She said, "Now, here, you see, it takes all the running you can do to keep in the same place. If you want to get somewhere else, you must run at least twice as fast!" When Lewis Carroll penned this classic, he could very well have been counseling people on their careers. As we know, anyone who remains in the same place today will soon become obsolete.

Study successful professionals such as physicians, attorneys, and engineers, and you'll observe that they routinely attend seminars, read journals, and participate in continuing education. They keep abreast of the latest developments in their field, always striving to improve themselves. Whatever you do, I advise you to make a concerted effort to stay well informed and keep your skills sharply honed. This requires habit: put aside an hour or so every day to read about your industry. Isn't this is a small price for success? When you do succeed, you must never stop doing what made you successful. Those who think they're through with learning still have a lot to learn.

When committed to a lifelong self-improvement program, you'll find you seek out information that others dismiss. In time, you'll acquire a level of expertise in your field that will be apparent to all who know you. Your reputation will spread, and even strangers will hail you as a leader in your field.

As a headhunter, I can assure you that your self-education will pay off during an interview. Well-informed recruiters weed out those candidates who only talk the talk. You, however, will radiate self-confidence because wherever the interviewer leads you will be familiar territory. You'll be able to hold your own when discussing current events going on in your industry. You'll even predict the future with authority. Believe me, this will give you a decisive edge over other candidates.

8

Having a Game Plan

Having decided what you want to do with the rest of your life, you need a game plan. This, too, must be in writing so you'll have a clear, concise course. Many people think they have a game plan, but they haven't committed it to writing, so it's too wishy-washy to follow. Eventually, it becomes so vague they hardly remember it. They may talk about their game plan, but it's only a fantasy.

A game plan provides basic direction, but remember to allow room for change. There will be detours and unforeseen events along the road. By having your plan in writing, you have reference points by which to measure your progress. A good game plan maps out in detail what you must do to achieve your long-term goal. It also includes short-term goals because long-term goals are generally reached one step at a time. In other words, a long-term goal is really a series of short-term goals. For this reason, focus on the big picture. Writing out your game plan allows you to maintain that focus. A career path has both peaks and valleys. You'll soon learn that setbacks don't really matter unless you allow them to defeat you. As somebody once said, "The secret to success is being able to have failure after failure without failing.

Remember this when you interview: it's not the end of the world if you don't get a job offer. Appreciate each opportunity to look at and remember who you are. The more confident and relaxed you are, the better your chances of doing well. Know that it's only a matter of time before you reach your goal—if this company doesn't want you, another will. You only need one job. Don't allow room for defeat and nothing can defeat you.

During interviews, you will be judged by how well you articulate your goals as well as how you plan to achieve them. You don't need a lot of details, but you should persuade the interviewer that you are thoughtful and strongly goal oriented.

A mechanical engineer had 12 years' experience in the refrigeration industry but didn't see a future with his employer. "My company hasn't developed a new product in seven years," he sighed, "and my job is unexciting."

He interviewed for a lateral position, seeking a higher base pay with more long-term opportunity. This, too, was for a refrigeration company, and it had two openings: one for an experienced mechanical engineer and another for a chief engineer. During a second interview, he spent an hour with the vice president of engineering, who asked, "Where do you want to be five years from now?"

The engineer replied that he wanted to be chief engineer in two years. "I believe I have the skills and the motivation to do the job," he emphasized.

During a third interview with the vice president, tests revealed the engineer had strong management potential and exceptional people skills. Two weeks later, he was offered the position of chief engineer and a 50 percent pay increase. This man attributed his interview success to his ability to articulate his long-range goals and his plans for achieving them.

9

Embrace Change

In cyberspace, time is measured in microseconds. Everything is subject to change with a single keystroke. Those who resist change will go the way of the dinosaur.

There is a natural tendency to oppose change because it entails the risk of making a wrong decision. People prefer to procrastinate because doing nothing is easier than taking action. However, sitting on the fence is a decision—they decided to do nothing!

Granted, deciding to change jobs is stressful. Psychologists rank the stress of changing jobs right up there with divorce and serious illness. It's stressful because most of us do it so rarely. Some people change jobs only once or twice in an entire career. And traditionally, our culture has frowned upon leaving one's job. Going back to pioneer days, Americans look down their noses at quitters.

It isn't necessary for me to explain when a job change seems in order. I assume you wouldn't be reading this book unless you already knew. Reasons may run the gamut, but it's never a welcome task.

During the interview, however, it is important that you appear to embrace change. Prospective employers know that, in today's business world, change is constant. Candidates who appear to resist change are viewed as indecisive or, worse, dated. Preferably, you will come across as a take-charge person—someone who will step up to the plate and meet challenges head-on.

1 0

Don't Allow Rejection to Defeat You

O nce you have decided on a career change, be prepared to face rejection. You're entering a highly competitive realm. There will be times when you'll compete against several other highly qualified candidates for the same position. That means somebody won't get hired. You may find the odds of getting the job are completely against you. Nonetheless, you must not allow rejection to defeat you. Fortunately, there are plenty of dream jobs to go around. If you strike out with one, you just keep right on swinging until you hit a home run.

Speaking of home runs, did you know that Babe Ruth at one time held the record for the most strikeouts? That's right, the Sultan of Swat, who hit 714 homers, went down swinging 1330 times.

Certainly, nobody likes rejection, but true champions in any field understand it's part of the game. I often see top executives face rejection several times before being accepted to even better jobs than the ones they lost! These are the real champions, the men and women who go on to be star performers when they do land their dream job. After all, it takes a lot of tenacity to muster up the enthusiasm and conviction required to go through an extensive interviewing process after having previously failed to make the final cut.

People who give up after losing a round or two confirm that they didn't deserve the job in the first place. After all, rejection is a fact of life—we all have to deal with it from time to time. Rarely do candidates have three interviews and receive three job offers. It hurts to be passed over, especially if you're unemployed. Just the same, you must look adversity in the eye without blinking. Now is the time to pump your-self up with self-confidence. Rid yourself of all your negative thoughts and fill your mind with positive ones. You must believe in yourself because only then can you convince others to believe in you.

It's understandable why people who are turned down for a desirable job take the rejection personally. But it's really nothing personal. All sorts of reasons exist that you can't possibly fathom—circumstances that have nothing to do with you! For example, the "hometown boy" may have an advantage over the out-of-town prospective employee. One survey shows that 76 percent of companies consider relocation expenses when making a hiring decision. Seventy-three percent indicate they'd choose a less qualified candidate who is local over a more quali-fied candidate who would have to relocate. This means that you may be playing against a stacked deck if you live on the west coast and the company and other candidates are based in New York City. Similarly, perhaps the company had a policy to meet all outside applicants even though an insider was a shoo-in. It's also possible that, after your interview, the company called an immediate hiring freeze. You can't dwell on rejection or your negative feelings will carry over to the next job interview.

For the sake of argument, let's say it *was* personal. What if the inter-viewer simply didn't like you? Maybe you look too much like her ex-husband, or, for that matter, a former boss who gave her a rough time. You can't sell 'em all, and if you haven't learned this lesson by now, it's time you did! Accept the fact that some people like vanilla ice cream and other people like chocolate ice cream.

Lee Iacocca has described being fired by Henry Ford, the CEO of Ford Motor Company. At the time, Iacocca had been the president of Ford for eight years. Having been told that Ford had asked for his resig-nation, Iacocca confronted him. "What's this all about?"

"It's personal," Ford replied, "and I can't tell you more. It's just one of those things."

Iacocca persisted, demanding Ford give him an answer. "Well, sometimes you just don't like somebody," Ford said.

Iacocca was devastated. However, he vowed not to get mad, but to get even. Later, as CEO of Chrysler, Iacocca transformed a dying company into one of America's greatest success stories. Lesser men would have been destroyed by such a brutal dismissal. True champions, however, are able to channel such incidents into opportunities—for self-examination, a tightening of focus, and a renewal of determination. They can look a temporary setback in the eye without letting it defeat them.

1 1

The Magic of Believing in Yourself

O kay, now that you're armed against rejection, you must approach every interview with a positive attitude. You must believe in yourself so strongly that you are convinced the job is yours if you want it. That's right, you must say, "The job is mine."

Now I'll caution you about coming across as "too confident." There's a thin line between confidence and arrogance. If you're perceived as too sure of yourself, you'll turn people off. Of course, you want to avoid self-deprecation and false modesty. Somewhere in between is the happy medium that shows recruiters you believe in yourself and yet are humble enough to listen and learn.

To win people, you must believe in yourself, or no one else will. When you go after something knowing you can have it, you will ooze with self-confidence. You will appear to be comfortable with yourself, and other people will feel comfortable with you. They'll be impressed, even if they can't say why. An interviewer might say, "I don't know why, but this person is right for the job. There's just something about her that says she'll get the job done."

They can't articulate the source of their impressions because you've communicated something subliminally. It's reflected in your tone of voice, speech patterns, facial expressions, and body language. By the way, it's something you can't fake—it has to be real.

So how can you do this? First, be certain you are qualified for the job you are seeking. You must be realistic—seeking and landing a job that's over your head is not smart. It's wonderful to believe in yourself, but be patient, and don't rush your career. Then, do your homework thoroughly. You want to feel totally prepared for anything that might be thrown at you. Finally, convince yourself that you're the best person for the job, because you are. If this seems difficult, review your journal of accomplishments. Think about your extraordinary achievements throughout your career. And talk to your biggest fans—people who think you walk on water! One last tip—give yourself a pep talk. Look into a mirror and see how right you are!

1 2

You Only Need One Job

Prepare yourself for several interviews, and factor in the possibility of rejection. Then believe in yourself, understanding you don't need a job offer with every interview. You only need one offer because you only need one job. Get it, and your mission is accomplished.

When it's all said and done, a score of prospective employers could pass on you (or you could pass on them). When somebody makes an offer too good to pass up, then your job search is over.

Eventually, everyone gets an offer. Look around you. Opportunities are everywhere. Eventually one will knock, and you'll answer.

I can recall hundreds of times when a job candidate was devastated after being turned down, only to get a better offer at the next interview. This happens so frequently, I sometimes tell candidates to look at rejection as "a blessing in disguise." I tell them, "Something better will come along, and someday you'll wonder why you even considered this position in the first place." It's amazing how often things turn out this way.

1 3

Beware of Doomsayers

Planning a career change is a big step, so it's likely you'll seek advice from those closest to you—family members, friends, and business associates. By all means, welcome their feedback, but take it with a grain of salt. Some will try to talk you out of it—for your own good.

Why? Not because they don't want you to be successful. Believe me, except for those who are jealous or fearful, they simply want to protect you. They're trying to save you from what they believe to be a major mistake. To most people, changing jobs for any reason is a bad idea.

Let's analyze this. For starters, there's the school of thought that says once you start something, you should finish it. Changing jobs is a sign of failure. Many old-timers remember tough times of high unemployment. They recall when jobs were hard to come by, and how the newly hired were the first to go during layoffs. To these people, changing jobs is never wise.

Next, there are those who resist any change, no matter what. They embrace routine and are alarmed by the uncertainty of change. This culture knows no age limits—it includes young and old alike.

There are also those who are so security conscious that they are paralyzed by fear of the unknown. "You know what you've got with your present job," they insist. "Who knows what a new job might bring!" Of course, false security is a bad thing, and serious problems with your present job should never be tolerated. Unfortunately, some people expect frustration and boredom as part of the job. They do not realize how much better life could be with a different employer.

Remember, too, family members and friends knew you "way back when." They look at you as the kid who delivered groceries or mowed the grass. They don't see you as the professional you have become. So your big ambitions may seem unrealistic to them. "So, you're a big shot now? Well, I remember babysitting for you and your sister after school!"

The truth is, these individuals know very little about you or your career, so they're not in a position to advise you. Think twice about their point of reference. The same applies for all unsolicited advice—and there will be plenty of it. Keep in mind that most people have your best interests at heart. And because they speak with such conviction, it's all the more difficult to separate the wheat from the chaff.

In summary, it's wise to seek advice from others. Just make sure your sources are well informed. Most importantly, shield yourself from what the doomsayers have to say. This is a time in your life when you need strong, positive, constructive feedback. You have enough uncertainty to overcome without going out and looking for more!

14

Be Prepared

For you ex-scouts out there, "be prepared" is more than just a motto for shaping resourceful, earnest, young citizens. After all, there is life beyond merit badges. As a matter of fact, being prepared is essential to anyone in the thick of a job search.

You would think that everyone knows the importance of going to an interview properly prepared. Not so! In fact, many candidates are so inadequately prepared that it's embarrassing. It's as if they think all they have to do is show up to get a job offer. This is why I refuse to take for granted this important aspect of the job search.

Of course, there are dozens of ways to prepare yourself for an interview, which is the focus of this first section. Just the same, it's here in print so nobody can say it wasn't included: *be prepared!*

You must do your homework before every interview. In my opinion, walking in unprepared is both presumptuous and disrespectful to the interviewer. You've wasted his or her time! Plus, asking ignorant questions about the company makes you look like a fool. Any savvy interviewer will think, "This person is a jerk!"

This is not the impression you want to want to make—and it's a sure way to eliminate yourself! Conversely, candidates who walk in fully prepared are the ones who shine. They do their homework in advance, and it gives them the confidence to ask appropriate questions and comment intelligently on the answers. Candidates who think they can bluff their way through an interview never do. In an interview, you need every advantage you can get. Being prepared gives you a leg up on your competition.

1 5

Investigate the Company

I can't imagine going to an interview without knowing about the company. Don't be surprised if the interviewer's first question is: "What do you know about us?" Walking in with little prior knowledge about your target company is foolhardy. Fortunately, there are some very good methods for obtaining information.

No matter what company you're courting—and this includes Coca-Cola and IBM—you have to do your homework. Don't assume that a company with a marquee name holds no surprises. Check it out thoroughly. The same applies to small, privately held companies. Investigate every company.

Start by checking every possible public source of information. The public library and the Internet are the best places to start. There, you can read current and past annual reports, as well as the company's detailed 10-K report, which every publicly owned corporation must file with the Securities and Exchange Commission (SEC). If an annual report or 10-K isn't available at the library, you can obtain them from your stockbroker or request them from the company. These reports are public information. While few people read them cover to cover, they contain significant data that you should know. At the very least, you should get a handle on how well the stock has traded over the previous 12-month period. If the subject comes up during your interview, you'll seem disinterested if you're in the dark.

Also, read as many magazine and newspaper articles as you can find on the company. Here you'll get pertinent facts about the industry, as well as financial analysts' views of the company's future. You'll pick up tidbits about high-ranking executives who may be profiled.

Researching a privately owned company is obviously more difficult because it is not required to provide public information. Nonetheless, sources such as Dun & Bradstreet or the local Chamber of Commerce may help you.

Be sure to investigate the company's major competitors. Knowing about the competition can be just as valuable as knowing about the company. Knowledge in this area is sure to impress the interviewer. Better yet, find out what the competition has to say about the company.

16

Research Via the Internet

We live in an incredible age. Today, grade-schoolers as well as professional writers are using the Internet for research. Volumes of information are right at our fingertips!

To get started, find the company's web site. Here you can review the company's annual report, 10-K, and investment prospectus. Don't simply glance at this information, analyze it carefully. You'll discover things about the company that many of its employees probably don't know. For instance, the 10-K will mention legal proceedings and awards that you can research further online. While you may not want to mention these subjects at an interview, you will get a feel for the company. The prospectus contains data on top management salaries and bonuses, including their stock options. It also profiles senior executives, including their backgrounds.

Be sure to read the company's mission statement as well as its values and principles. Not only will you uncover the organization's personality, you may want to refer to it during the interview.

You can also search the Internet for newspaper and magazine articles. Of course, what's available will differ from one company to another. Some get more coverage than others. Starting with the most current, thoroughly read as many articles as you can find. If only excerpts are available, track down the complete story at the library. For even more insight, read about the industry itself, as well as about the competition.

One excellent place to get a good company profile is Hoovers.com. Then there's Edgar's Online Service, which covers everything from SEC filings to stock market activity. Use search engines such as Hotbot,

Yahoo, MSN, and Alta Vista. And be sure to visit MSN Investor, Bloomberg, DOW, Fidelity, Smith Barney, Goldman Sachs, Morningstar, and Value Lines. Last but not least, visit The Motley Fool chat room.

Some companies have such an abundance of coverage that you'll sift through it for hours. You may not have time to read everything; absorb as much as you can.

1 7

What's the Company Culture?

I t brings tears to my eyes to hear about someone who landed a dream job only to shortly begin another search. "It was a bad cultural fit," she laments.

Culture varies as much from company to company as from country to country. It's the biggest influence on how you'll fit in. Examine the Big Five accounting firms PriceWaterhouseCoopers, Deloitte&Touche, etc. Each offers the same service and skills as its competition. Each leases offices and equipment. Even employees seem the same from one firm to another. Plus, they spew out pretty much the same work—even their job specs are similar. So what makes one an ideal place to work? It's likely the culture difference—a person may feel comfortable at one firm and not at another.

Job candidates must never underestimate the significance of a company's culture. There's no guarantee you will simply adjust to a new corporate environment. You must get a firm grip on company culture very early in your search. This serves two purposes. First, you'll save a lot of time. You'll know you'd be better off elsewhere and move on. Second, you'll be better equipped to land the position you want. Keep in mind that you'll spend most of your waking hours working at your new company. Make sure this is where you want to be for the next umpteen years.

So how do you educate yourself about the company culture before the interview? Again, start with the library or the company's web page. Read up on their key people. Find out where they're from, what schools they attended, and so on.

See if you can determine diversity. Is the company a melting pot? Does it have a high turnover of top executives? Have there been recent takeovers or management shake-ups? Find out about a new leader's personality and style. Whom has he brought with him?

Is the company a good corporate citizen? Is senior management involved in the community? Does the company demonstrate a concern for people in general?

Local citizens will have stories about large employers. It's worth talking to them; the cost of a few long-distance calls may save you money in the end. Or, you can drop into local Internet chat rooms and ask around.

What is the company's focus? What is its niche? What are its priorities? In what direction is it moving? What do present and former employees have to say about the company? What do customers say?

As you learn about the company culture, you'll get a taste of what it's like before your interview. If it's not to your liking, you may as well pass on it!

18

Talk to Present
and Former Employees

If you personally know anyone who works at XYZ Company, see what she has to say about the company. Even if your contact is only entry level, you'll get some valuable feedback. She'll know firsthand how managers treat subordinates. In fact, sometimes you can learn more from rank-and-file employees than from senior people. A shipping clerk might say, "Everybody is so friendly around here. Why, just the other day, the CEO dropped in and asked how we'd solve a problem."

Conversely, a programmer might say, "I have a lot of ideas, but nobody ever listens to me. What the hell. I just do what I'm paid to do."

Employees probably won't volunteer this sort of information, so you'll have to ask the right questions. "Does your company ever ask you for suggestions? Do you ever offer them? Are they receptive when you do? Have you ever suggested something that they implemented?" If you ask questions of this nature, people will open up about the company.

Current employees may refrain from saying anything negative because they fear reprisal, or simply because they don't want to bite the hand that feeds them. So seek out ex-employees, too. Chances are, they'll be more candid. However, former employees sometimes have a chip on their shoulder. Someone who got canned is likely to have a jaundiced view. Hear him out, but talk to several people before forming an opinion. Remember, there are always three sides to every story!

Here, too, you can search the Web for former employees. If you consistently get negative feedback, you can conclude that where there's smoke, there's fire.

You might even consider going where company employees gather for lunch or happy hour. It's amazing what you can pick up during casual conversations.

Both former and current employees attend trade shows and association meetings. Blind calls to Customer Service, Sales, Subscriptions, and Personnel are also good ways to get a feel for a company.

For obvious reasons, it's better to talk to an employee you know or to one who has been recommended by a third party. But sometimes this isn't an option. Let's say you're not using a search firm. (In Tip #30, "Why a Headhunter?" I'll further explain why you should use one). There is nothing wrong with calling the receptionist to say, "I'm coming in on Thursday for an interview. Your company looks like it has just what I'm looking for. I want to do my best, so I'd like to ask you a few questions about the company."

Even if you "cold call" employees, as long as you're friendly, many of them will give you basic information. Again, don't expect them to say anything negative. Surprisingly, however, some employees will be candid and will say whatever is on their mind.

Don't be concerned if the interviewer learns you've been investigating the company. She won't be offended. In fact, most managers will admire your assertiveness because it demonstrates your interest and initiative. If a company resents your curiosity, it's probably not the place for you.

1 9

Talk to Customers and Vendors

Vendors can tell you what it's like doing business with the company. Unlike an employee, their perspective is from the outside looking in.

One large department store consistently puts people on hold when they call the home office. Sales representatives complain of waiting hours to meet with buyers. One rep says, "I dread going there because they treat people like dirt."

This particular company's reputation for disrespect begins internally; its own people keep each other waiting for meetings.

Customers are easier to reach than employees because there are typically more of them. Furthermore, they have nothing to lose by talking with you. Customer service is central to the personality of a company. Regardless of age or stature, all companies should go that extra mile for their customers. Don't assume that they all do. You'll discover some companies have terrible reputations for customer service. You'll hear horror stories of people fighting tooth and nail to get what they're due under service agreements. You'll hear complaints about shipping and false warranties. No matter how well this company may treat employees, will you be able to sleep at night knowing customers get raked over the coals? Of course, companies that treat their customers shabbily generally do likewise with employees.

20

Familiarize Yourself with the Product

If you were attending a dinner party where a famous author would be guest of honor, you'd probably read at least one of his books beforehand.

A job candidate should extend the same consideration by checking out the product prior to an interview. Brush your teeth with their toothpaste, test drive one of their cars, or talk to people who use the product. Candidates can't bluff their way through an interview, especially when it comes to this kind of experience.

Prior to an interview with Disney World, spend an afternoon at the park. No amount of other research will be able to replace the "Disney experience." Walk the floor of a retail outlet to get a feel of the shopping experience from the customer's point of view. Nothing beats hands-on information about how the product works, or how it is made and sold.

Attend trade shows and talk to customers, sales reps, and even competitors. Ask tough questions about the product's weaknesses as well as its strengths. If this isn't feasible, read as much company sales literature as you can find.

You're not expected to become an expert on the product. No matter how much you study, you won't know as much as the interviewer. You don't have to know everything to come across as well informed. Just don't walk in cold.

Don't be shy about asking questions. It's okay to ask why a particular product failed. Just don't dwell on it. And while you're at it, be sure to ask what's on the drawing board.

21

Check Out
the Interviewer

During the interview, the most important person in the company is sitting across the desk from you. Just as you investigated the company and its product, you must also check out the interviewer.

A high-profile CEO of a *Fortune 500* company is relatively easy to research. You can read about him in magazines and trade articles, review his comments in annual reports, and even see a profile on the company's web site. Hoovers.com is an excellent source for executive profiles. But you're probably not going to be interviewed by a *Fortune 500* CEO.

The farther down the corporate ladder you go, the leaner the information. Forget about published articles. There aren't any. The company's web site might not even mention the interviewer's name, but don't despair. There are other ways to find out what you need to know.

Simply call the company and ask the receptionist about him. This approach is so obvious that most candidates overlook it. Just say, "Hello, my name is John Miller, and I'm meeting with Bill Smith on Thursday at 2:00. I would really like to join ABC Company. Do you mind if I ask you a few questions about Mr. Smith? It would really make the interview go a lot smoother."

If you get a positive response, proceed.

"What is he like? His style, his demeanor. Is he a laid-back, casual type of person, or is he one of those let's-get-right-down-to-business types? What's his background? Did he always work for ABC Company? If not, where did he come from?

"How long has he been with the company? What is his specific job? What kind of projects has he worked on in the past? Where did he go to school? What are his outside interests?" In most cases, pleasant questions of this nature will get you helpful answers.

Candidates sometimes ask me, "Isn't this a little too aggressive? What if it gets back to the interviewer that I was prying into his affairs?"

Again, the majority of interviewers will admire your assertiveness. You've demonstrated initiative, which separates you from other candidates.

2 2

Call the Interviewer

The most direct way to find out what the interviewer is like is to call him.

"Hello, Mr. Smith, this is John Miller. I'm calling to confirm tomorrow's 10:30 interview. Is there anything in particular that you would like me to prepare for tomorrow morning?"

"I'm glad you called, John. Could you bring me your reviews from your former boss?"

"I certainly will. Is there anything else you'd like?"

"That's all, John. I'm looking forward to seeing you tomorrow."

"Same here. Say, how long have you been with the company?"

"I've been here for eight years."

"Really? Where did you come from?"

You can see where this is heading. It's easy to get into a conversation with the interviewer, and, as a result, pick up some valuable clues. Keep it friendly and polite. But be subtle. If you gush or patronize, or you'll seem insincere—or, even worse, devious.

23

The Door Opener—
Your Résumé

Ideally, a well-written résumé should whet the appetite of the inter-viewer. But remember: it's an appetizer, not a full-course meal.

Your résumé is usually your first contact with a recruiter. It creates an impression of you before you've even walked in the door.

Make sure your résumé is printed from a computer. This way, it's crisp and clean, and signals that you're computer literate and ready for the twenty-first century. A résumé written by hand or typed on an old Underwood speaks volumes about your capabilities—specifically, your lack of them.

If candidates were hired solely on the merits of their résumés, there would be no need for interviews. A great résumé won't guarantee you a dream job, but a sloppy, poorly written one will disqualify you from getting an interview, no matter how qualified you may be. Recruiters with tight schedules eliminate candidates who submit unkempt and ill-prepared résumés. First and foremost, your résumé must capture the reader's attention. Make sure it's aesthetically pleasing and not cluttered. Tailor your résumé to what the interviewer is seeking. Remember: the résumé gets you the interview—not the job!

Don't misinterpret—content is crucial. But if presentation is poor, substance won't matter because your résumé won't even be read.

Whether you're applying for a sales, management, or administrative position, a well-written résumé demonstrates your communication skills—a must in today's job market. Your résumé tells the interviewer whether you have these skills.

2 4

The Format of a Well-Written Résumé

Even though experts disagree on what constitutes a good résumé, within the recruiting industry there is a consensus. First, let me tell you a few things about hiring authorities. They have tight work schedules and are pressed for time. They review many résumés and don't spend a lot of time reading them. They abhor résumés that are lengthy, improperly written or boring, that is, those with a lot of text. My advice: don't make them read a lot—and don't put them to sleep!

Thanks to personal computers, formatting a résumé has never been easier. There are literally shelves of "how-to" books at bookstores and libraries, so take the time to review some. Photocopy a few sample résumés that appeal to you. But be sure your finished résumé isn't straight out of the book—interviewers don't want cookie-cutter résumés. Use book examples as guides.

Keep in mind the importance of eye appeal when selecting a style. Make sure it passes the 20-second test—most hiring executives have so little time that 20 seconds is about all you get to make an impression. Try to limit your résumé to a single page. Two pages is permissible, but don't make it longer!

Pay close attention to details. For instance, I recommend margins between three-fourths of an inch to one inch on the sides, top, and bottom. The font size should be about 12 points, but your name should be larger—14 to 16 points. Use plain white paper only. Tinted paper doesn't copy well. Frequently, résumés are copied and distributed to several people.

For legibility, break up text with headings in boldface. Use italics for subheadings or for emphasis within a paragraph.

Example 1
Area Manager, SmithKline Beecham
Supervisor for 20 field sales representatives

Example 2
Boosted Big Three sales (*The Home Depot, Lowe's, HQ*) by 30 percent.

Break a series of thoughts into a list, such as career highlights, and use bullet points to indent them. Bullets themselves should be details rather than complete sentences.

Correct
• Company's 1998–1999 number one salesperson in software division.

Incorrect
• I was the company's top software salesperson in 1998–1999.

Limit your use of bullets and bold and italic print—they should highlight your achievements. Too much is distracting.

Appearance is essential, but naturally the content of your résumé counts most. You want to detail your experience and education in a unique way. You must be precise and factual, with your name, address, phone number, fax number, and e-mail address at the top, followed by your career objective and a summary of qualifications. Your work history follows, in reverse chronological order. You shouldn't go back too far if you've held a lot of jobs; 10 years is adequate. But if you had only two or three jobs in 25 years, you should include them all. It's not necessary to include the dates of multiple jobs with the same company. Simply mention the dates that you were with that company. Next comes your education, which is less important if you have lots of experience. However, candidates under 30 without a track record should list education under summary of qualifications.

Your résumé should be financial-driven. This means that when describing different positions throughout your career, show how you made or saved money for your employers. The bottom line is what turns on hiring authorities. This quantifies your accomplishments.

Either include references with your résumé, or don't mention them until the interview. Personally, I don't like résumés that say, "References upon request." This looks as if the candidate has something to hide. As a rule of thumb, the higher up the corporate ladder, the less important references will be on a résumé.

25

Résumé References

It isn't necessary for a candidate for CEO with a *Fortune 500* company to give references. Be assured, however, that the hiring company will thoroughly investigate the candidate, leaving no stone unturned.

However, let's say you include references on your résumé. I recommend listing six. Two should be former employers, preferably your immediate boss or the boss's boss, two peers, and two subordinates. Any of these can be people you've worked with. If you don't have these six references, you can list a client—but only as a last resort. Be sure to include titles, addresses, and phone numbers of your references.

You should always notify a person you're using as a reference. It's essential to have their permission. It's also important that they're not caught off guard. If they don't know you're using them as a reference, they might not return the hiring authority's call!

Ask these individuals to write a reference letter for you—it's okay to coach them on what you think they should mention. Take these letters to the interview. You may also mention the letters in your cover letter, but not in your résumé.

Hiring authorities know that people only list references who will say good things about them. They will always contact them anyway. So be selective about the references you choose—they will definitely make a difference.

2 6

Proofreading Your Résumé

A single typographical error or misspelled word can ruin an otherwise perfect résumé. When dozens of candidates compete for the same job, one typo can dispatch a résumé directly to the trash.

"Do you mean that something as insignificant as a typo could eliminate me from the running? Are you telling me that my entire life could be irrevocably altered because I used a comma instead of a semicolon?"

In a word, *yes.*

Hiring authorities tell me that spelling and grammatical errors tend to jump off the page. People who read a lot of résumés pick up on these faux pas, rarely letting one go unnoticed. It's not the improper punctuation that will be your demise, it's the message this sends. By not proofreading your résumé, you show that you didn't properly prepare yourself. This indicates that you don't pay attention to details.

Don't rely on the spell-check feature of your computer, either. It won't pick up on homonyms such as "its" and "it's" or "their" and "there," or know that you meant "his" instead of "him," or "her" instead of "he." Chances are you'll overlook a few mistakes after preparing and reading your own writing. After you've proofread your résumé, have someone with good writing skills review it. Even professional writers have writer's assistants and proofreaders.

27

What to Do about Those Gaps in Your Résumé

Employment gaps jump off the page of a résumé. Experienced recruiters quickly spot them, so it's important you know what to do.

Some gaps can't be avoided. Good people get sick, have children, are downsized, and so on. Good workers are also fired—but it doesn't automatically mean they deserved it. Remember, Ford Motor Company fired Lee Iacocca.

It's permissible to bury small gaps in your résumé. For instance, if you were let go on April 25 and started your next job on June 15, it's okay to say your employment ended in May and your next employer hired you in June. Large gaps, however, must be explained. If the hiring authority checks your references and finds that you covered up six months of unemployment, you'll ruin your chances. You might be able to hide several gaps by listing years instead of specific months. But if the gap is between your last job and the present, be sure to explain it in your cover letter.

Honesty is the best policy. Don't get too "creative" with the truth. Generally, it all comes out in the wash.

Recruiters understand that during periods of weak economy, good jobs are hard to find. They also realize that people who perform well become victims of circumstances beyond their control. Companies merge, corporate culture changes, and a new boss with an agenda can result in your termination.

Likewise, taking time off to be a full-time parent is a valid reason for a two- or three-year gap. However, be sure to specify in your résumé why you weren't working. Put down "1992–1993 Maternity leave and family management," or "1994–1995 Travel and full-time student."

If you have a chopped-up work history with many short-term jobs, try to combine some under a single heading, especially if they go back several years. You might have worked for several insurance companies, retail stores, and real estate agencies during a period, but this is not something you want to identify. Omit some of the less important, briefer jobs: "1986–1992 Sales—insurance, retailing, and real estate." If you're over 40, and you think age discrimination might work against you, don't go back so far in time that you automatically date yourself. Keep in mind that you don't have to include your entire work history—especially what you did 30 years ago!

As an alternative to explaining a gap in the body of your résumé, you can mention it in your cover letter. However, if there's a gap because you took a sabbatical and traveled in Europe or worked in community services—something of interest to potential employers—include this in your résumé.

2 8

11 Fatal Errors
in a Résumé

We've seen a lot of résumés at MRI. At my request, our head-hunters submitted what they thought were the most common faux pas. The following are fatal errors in a résumé:

- *Poor grammar, typos, misspellings, etc.* A sloppy résumé says you're careless.

- *Overkill.* Anything over a page-and-a-half is too long.

- *Vagueness.* Quantify your results. Don't state: "Responsible for supervising 300 employees." Instead, say: "Managed the marketing department that increased revenues 82 percent in a four-year period." Don't write a job description; list what you have accomplished.

- *Plagiarism.* Avoid patterning your résumé after the same examples everyone else uses. Hiring authorities get bored with look-alike résumés. Be creative and different—but only to a point.

- *Colored paper.* Any color other than white paper is unacceptable. Colored paper does not copy well—your résumé will be distributed to multiple people.

- *Clichés and buzzwords.* Don't use words that you think sound "smart." Hiring authorities are not impressed with "utilize," "flexible," "team player," and "seeking an opportunity for me to grow and develop."

- *Tiresome details.* If you're well into your career, skip those college summer jobs. As you advance in age and up the corporate ladder, pare down your résumé. Nobody really cares that you worked your way through college waiting tables, especially when you're applying for an executive position with a securities firm.

- *Indeterminate gender.* If you're Pat, Lynn, or Lee, don't keep 'em guessing. With certain names, use Mr. or Ms. as a prefix.

- *Lying.* First, you don't lie because it's wrong. Second, you don't lie because if you get caught, you won't get the job.

- *Omitting your job objective.* State clearly what you're looking for. Ambiguity indicates you lack direction and focus.

- *Listing your job objective.* Note that this contradicts the previous point. Some headhunters think a job objective limits the candidate. If the exact position isn't available within the organization, the candidate automatically eliminates himself from a job. Do your homework in advance to be sure your objective coincides with an open position before including it in the résumé. If there are several positions that interest you, do not include your objective.

Visit MRI's website, BrilliantPeople.com, for more tips on putting together an effective résumé.

29

The Résumé Cover Letter

Nobody ever landed a job because of an incredibly written cover letter, but I can personally tell you about otherwise strong candidates who wrote terrible letters and were automatically eliminated. For this reason, many headhunters think a well-written cover letter is as important as the résumé itself.

When you send out your résumé, it must always be accompanied by a letter. There are no exceptions. Even when somebody says, "Just drop off your résumé to me in an envelope or fax it to my attention—don't bother with a cover letter." You still send one. If you don't, someone else in the hiring chain will think you're either lazy or professionally clumsy. Either way, you're off to a bad start.

First impressions are made with the cover letter. In the search business, we think good first impressions are vital. You may have the best background, but a weak cover letter can land your résumé in the trash basket.

A well-written cover letter is professional, is properly formatted, and gets right to the point. Let me emphasize being professional. Don't get folksy or cutesy. Be brief, and don't use flowery words, cliches, or jargon. Avoid sounding stiff, and maintain a balance between professionalism and friendliness. Each letter should be tailor-made to the company. But don't go overboard—just make it sound like you didn't pick this company out of the yellow pages. Perhaps most important is to mention how you were referred to the company, if, indeed, you were referred (that is, "Bill Brown suggested I contact you . . ." "I am responding to posting.")

Again, if there are obvious gaps in your employment, provide a brief explanation. But keep it short. Hiring authorities don't like to read a long cover letter.

3 0

Why a Headhunter?

Because I'm founder and chairman of the board of the world's largest headhunting firm, you might think I have ulterior motives for recommending a search firm. The truth is, there are so many compelling reasons for working with a headhunter that I could write a book on the subject!

The higher up the corporate ladder you go, the more likely your prospective company will rely on a search firm. If you're looking for a position in the executive suite, you definitely should be working with a headhunter. In case you didn't know, the hiring company pays the fee— a headhunter's services don't cost you anything. With that obstacle removed, let's look at why you should consider a headhunter.

A headhunter is engaged by a client (the company that has a position open for a specific employee), which pays him a fee comparable to about 30 percent of the placed employee's first-year salary. The headhunter then contacts prospects. This means that many of the best jobs are available only through a headhunter. If you're not working with one, you won't know about these positions.

Nearly all candidates that headhunters contact are already employed. Simply put, individuals currently working are more desirable to hiring authorities. This doesn't automatically make them the most qualified. But it's generally believed that if you're presently working, you have more to offer than somebody who quit, was laid off, or fired. Of course, wooing people who are satisfied with their jobs and are not contemplating a career move is not easy. Headhunters frequently must convince a perfectly content employee to switch jobs—somebody who woke up that morning without the faintest notion of leaving his present employer. Headhunters must entice this person to "look into an exciting opportunity."

A headhunter might say, "It doesn't hurt to see what's out there." This is true. It doesn't hurt to see what other companies are paying people in positions similar to yours. And who knows what might be available to sweeten the deal? Oftentimes, people employed for years at a company discover they are significantly underpaid. However, never having learned the going rate for their services, they are unaware of such disparities. So, even though you're completely satisfied, there's no harm in just talking. Who knows, you may discover you're worth more to your company than the going rate—this may help you in your next round of salary negotiations. By the way, a majority of our placements are people who are not in the market but who are willing to "take a look." Evidently, if these individuals were unable to find significantly better jobs, it would be difficult for my company to stay in business.

For some people who never considered making a job change, that first call from a headhunter is a godsend. After all, here's a person who's been keeping his nose to the grindstone and doesn't have the faintest clue what's available. Suddenly, a headhunter provides this individual with an immense job opportunity. In my opinion, this is a wonderful service. When everything falls into place, it's a great feeling.

One advantage to the hiring company is that headhunters "weed out" weak prospects. Getting sent only the best candidates saves a firm's hiring authorities a lot of time, and they know this assures them of better people to interview. Obviously, this works to your advantage, too, because you've been approved by the headhunter. Keep in mind that search firms don't represent every candidate who walks through their doors. Generally, a headhunter takes on only one in every ten candidates. They screen them very carefully before dispatching them to a client.

There's a flip side to this. If a position is available and the headhunter has a dozen or so candidates better qualified than you, you won't get sent. On your own, however, you could approach the company and land the interview. A sincere headhunter will say, "I don't believe that I can assist you. In fact, I can hurt you. If I present you to a company that I have a contract with, you can't approach it on your own for any position for the next year. Perhaps you should consider seeing this company without my participation, so I don't hurt your chances." In addition, a headhunter with access to many executives more qualified than you may not promote you as a top candidate. You can, however, promote yourself as *your* number one candidate!

Note that seasoned headhunters have many years of experience. This means they have numerous contacts across the country. You can't possibly have as many—remember, contacting people is what they do! Most importantly, they have built relationships with their client companies over time. If you have been working for the same employer for many years, your network is extremely limited. Besides, headhunters are professionals. They work at this full time. You, on the other hand, are a novice at finding new and better jobs.

Of course, the most important service a headhunter provides is counseling. She can advise you on everything from how to prepare your résumé to what to wear to the interview. Since the headhunter is likely to have a history with the hiring company, the client, she can give you general background about the company such as corporate culture, track record, key decision makers, and competition. Headhunters will also have current literature on the company, including newsletters that may feature the person who will interview you. Here, the headhunter can save you time you'd have spent researching on your own. Most importantly, the headhunter personally knows the hiring authorities and can coach you on the right things to say to score points.

Following the interview, the headhunter can serve as a sounding board. She will review the interview with you, asking all sorts of questions such as "What did the interviewer say about the gaps in your résumé? How did you answer? Were you comfortable with your reply?

What questions did you ask?" The headhunter can put a positive spin on a so-so interview and can follow up by asking the interviewer, "What would it take for Kevin Miller to get the job?" At the very least, if you do poorly in an interview, a good headhunter can figure out where you goofed and coach you on how to do well the next time out. She serves as a great motivator. It can be awfully lonely trying to land a job on your own.

After the interview, a headhunter continues to earn her keep by acting as an intermediary between the hiring authority and the job candidate. The headhunter can monitor everything from closing the agreement to negotiating your salary. As you can see, headhunters provide a valuable service to both parties. No wonder most *Fortune 500* companies use them to find key employees.

3 1

Building Relationships with Headhunters *before* You Start Your Search

There are two choices when it comes to building relationships with headhunters: you can wait until you're on your way out of a job or you can start before you actually need them. Professionals who plan their careers don't wait until they are completely dissatisfied with their jobs. They understand that business constantly changes and there are no guarantees for the future. Even *Fortune 500* companies merge and go bankrupt.

Smart people realize the value of a strong relationship with a headhunter. If nothing else, it serves as a safety net. Even though a career change may be the farthest thing from your mind, when a good headhunter calls, hear him out.

Top headhunters are astute, and they know a lot about your industry. They're in constant contact with high-ranking executives, so they're a good source of information about your field. They also know the going rate that companies pay people in your line of work. So, even if you have no plans for a career switch, it's beneficial to know what you're worth.

Truly outstanding headhunters are terrific sounding boards. Although their objective is to place people in key positions, they're long-term thinkers. They understand that while you are not a serious candidate today, you may be in the future. They're interested in long-term relationships, too. Even though you agree to meet informally, if he's worth his salt, he'll say, "Now, I don't work for you. I work for the client. He's the person who pays my bill. I've got to have this commodity called the challenge, or human capital, and that's why I'm putting you in my database. If something comes along that I think is right for you, you're going to hear from me."

It doesn't matter that you don't intend to leave your present position; you should be grateful. Let's just say it's something for a rainy day! Another way to look at it is that you wouldn't wait until April 15 to meet with an accountant. Nor would you wait until you have a horrendous toothache before you visit a dentist. Smart people build relationships before desperate situations occur. Likewise, you should partner with a headhunter long before you need his services.

If you're in senior management and have headhunters contacting you in your role as hiring authority, don't brush them off too quickly. Even if you have no interest in their candidate, hear them out. You may someday need their services. I've seen executives who never even bother to get a headhunter's card. Down the road, they regret it.

3 2

Why Headhunters Hunt Almost Exclusively for Employed Individuals

Everybody knows it's tougher to find a job when you don't have one.

As stated, there are reasons why good people are unemployed. But hiring authorities like better odds, which favor going with an employed candidate. An unemployed individual is a red flag to recruiters—and signals an uphill battle for the headhunter. People without jobs are seen as the negative side of the coin.

First, an unemployed person is viewed as poorly organized. Otherwise, he would have anticipated his unemployment and not gotten stuck without a job. Companies see this person as inefficient. This stumbling block makes the headhunter's job harder.

Second, when an employed candidate leaves his company to join another, he is making a major commitment. He is walking away from a lucrative position with good benefits. The unemployed candidate isn't leaving anything, so he has virtually no risk.

Third, when a candidate is unemployed, the hiring authority is likely to offer a lower salary. Why? Because the candidate without income is viewed as desperate. There's also the "desirability factor"—people value what they can't have. If a recruiter has to lure away a candidate from a competitor, it's a real coup compared to hiring an unemployed person.

33

How to Sell Yourself to a Headhunter When You're Unemployed

Now that you know that unemployed candidates are less desirable, you can still approach headhunters differently if you're in between jobs. A bit of advice: Be prepared to explain convincingly why you're not employed.

For many of the same reasons that it's difficult to get a job when you're unemployed, it's harder to find a top headhunter who's willing to work with you.

Headhunters don't like unemployed candidates because they're harder to place. From a business perspective, headhunters have an inventory they must move. Candidates are their inventory. They must determine whether you are a marketable commodity. Once you understand this, your mindset must be "How can I position myself as a winning product?"

Successful headhunters already have qualified people to place. Unless you can convince them that you're a strong candidate, they don't want you. It's important for you to understand why being unemployed is considered undesirable. One reason is that an unemployed person is usually too aggressive, or, at the other extreme, too laid back. For instance, a senior executive who's been out of circulation for an extended period will tend to chatter and try to dominate the conversation during an interview. In truth, she's scared and lacks confidence, and she overcompensates by rattling on and on. Some are even belligerent and resist the headhunter's counseling. At the other extreme are those who look like they're about to fall to sleep.

Unemployed candidates have another strike against them. The hiring authority thinks, "There must be something wrong with him if he's unemployed." So how do you sell the headhunter when you're unemployed? First, ask yourself what will make you easier to sell. Most headhunters specialize in a particular industry, so it's important to approach one who will see you as a viable product because you're what he "sells." In other words, if a headhunter works with legal, accounting, and brokerage firms and you happen to be in pharmaceutical sales, you're probably going to strike out with him because he doesn't have a "buyer" for you.

Second, headhunters don't like merchandise that has already been shown. They'll assume that if you're unemployed, you've already circulated your résumé and called lots of recruiters. You must inform the headhunter that you're fresh goods. One of the first things you should say is, "I'm just beginning my search. I haven't contacted any other recruiters. In fact, I'd like to have an exclusive relationship with you for a time—that is, if you feel you can help me." A headhunter is more receptive to this candidate than to one who gives the impression she's talked to every recruiter in town.

Third, don't beat around the bush. Get right to the point about why you're unemployed. Start off by saying, "I'm out of work because . . ." Headhunters want this information early in their first conversation with you.

Fourth, successful headhunters are busy people. The easier you make things for them, the more desirable you'll be. They like proactive candidates who help with the research. Since you're currently unemployed, you have more time than the headhunter does to search the Internet and visit the library. You might provide her with a list of target companies that you like. By coming up with the names of hiring authorities and phone numbers, I can assure you that you'll score points with a headhunter.

3 4

Contingency Search Firms or Retained Search Firms?

Headhunters work for either a contingency search firm or a retained search firm. You should know the difference—which is basically the method by which fees are paid. The client pays a contingency search firm when a placement is made. If no one is hired, no fee is paid. It's like a salesperson working on straight commission or an attorney who receives a percentage of the settlement instead of charging an hourly fee. If the attorney doesn't win, she isn't paid.

As the name suggests, a retained search firm is paid a retainer. This means the client pays a fee up front plus expenses, including telephone and travel. Retained search firms sometimes conduct psychological testing on candidates, for which they are also reimbursed. Retained firms do not guarantee a hire.

A hybrid of these two types of firms occurs when a priority search is conducted by a contingency search firm. Here, the client pays one-third of the fee up front with the guarantee of a placement. The balance is paid only after a positive hire.

About 85 percent of all search firms work on a contingency basis. A retained search firm is more likely to be engaged for the highest level position placements, including CEOs of *Fortune 500* companies.

3 5

Interviewing the Headhunter

There are some things you need to know about talking with a head-hunter. Let's say a headhunter doing a search for his client contacts you. Hear him out, and don't be shy about asking questions. Assuming you've done your homework and are satisfied that he represents a reputable firm, ask about his area of specialty. Find out how much he knows about your industry. Try to determine how well connected he is. It's important that he knows key players in your industry.

Ask about the offer that he's brought you. Ask how he got your name. Reputable headhunters will not hesitate to tell you. Inquire if his firm is a member of the Association of Executive Search Consultants, which has a code of conduct for its members. Only after you have these answers can you decide if the job is worth pursuing.

If you're approaching the headhunter, this is an entirely different scenario. Be sure to ask, "Do you work with people with my background in this particular industry?" Also, ask, "Does your network go beyond your local geographical area?"

Then follow with, "I'd like to have a relationship with someone who networks with other recruiters on a confidential basis. I don't have time to talk to 10 good recruiters."

Don't think that you have a wonderful contact just because an old classmate or golf buddy is a headhunter. Unless he or she specializes in your field, you're likely to end up spinning your wheels. However, you might want to call this person for advice on how to get hooked up with the right headhunter.

Let's assume that you have now contacted a headhunter who specializes in your area and has clients with job opportunities for you. You must convince him that your experience qualifies you as a strong candidate. Begin by critiquing your job history. If you're unemployed, state exactly why. Be totally honest. Headhunters talk to candidates every day, and they've heard everything. Think of him as a state trooper who's pulled you over for speeding. Believe me, the trooper knows every excuse in the book. You're not going to talk him out of giving you a ticket.

Imagine someone telling a headhunter, "I was making $300,000 a year and got bored, so I quit my job three months ago and I'm looking for the right opportunity." Headhunters know that smart people rarely walk away from a job paying $6000 a week. People stay where they are until the right position is available—the headhunter would think this person is either lying or stupid! Either way, he shoots himself in the foot.

Once you've established that you're a good candidate, let the head-hunter know that you're anxious to work with him and will trust him to take charge of the search. Remember, headhunters like candidates who make their work easy, so ask, "What do you need from me?"

It's always appropriate to ask for references of clients or candidates. Inquire about candidates he's placed who are in your same earnings range. Be sure to follow up with calls to these people.

3 6

Things You Never Say to a Headhunter

"**H**ey, I'm calling to see if I could make you some money."

"I'm just testing the water, so I thought I'd give you a call."

We hear these dumb remarks every day, and nothing turns us off faster. Common sense should dictate why these are rude statements, but evidently some people don't have much common sense.

3 7

How to Keep Your Search Discreet

If you're employed and considering a job change, there's always the chance that your present employer will find out. There are certain precautions you can take, but there is no way to make yourself 100 percent immune to this risk.

Companies want to hire experienced people, so they like to hire employees away from their competitors. These people can hit the ground running. What makes this especially risky for candidates is that coworkers from your present company may have joined the competition and vice versa.

Executives also network at conventions and association meetings. They exchange information with each other at dinner and on the golf course. And they call each other for opinions on prospective employees. As a result, everybody knows everybody.

When you work with a headhunter, you can maintain a low profile. Your headhunter will respect your request to protect your confidentiality and emphasize utmost discretion to the hiring authority. She will use due diligence to shield your résumé from casual onlookers. Furthermore, she will seek your approval before contacting her clients on your behalf. Only with your permission will she set up an interview. She will not reveal your name until complete confidentiality has been assured. Correspondence will travel only via private fax machines or certified mail and courier services. Of course, no matter what a headhunter does, the risk of discovery can never be entirely eliminated. Nevertheless, if you're not working with a headhunter, the risk is even greater, and varies according to the sources you use to set up interviews. You never know whose blind post office box you're responding to— it might even belong to your own boss!

If you're working solo, you also have the right to request discretion. For the most part, human resources executives and hiring authorities will respect your wishes.

38

The Best and
Worst Ways
to Get Interviews

There are many ways to get time with a hiring authority—some are better than others. Obviously, you have a better chance if you're the boss' son-in-law than if you picket the building with a sign reading, "Hire me." In descending order, here are your best and worst chances:

Search firms/personal contacts
Referrals from coworkers or business associates
Job fairs/career centers
Newspaper advertising
College counseling services
Internet
State employment services
Unsolicited résumés/walk-ins/cold calls

3 9

Networking—
Who You Know
Can Help

Personal contacts and search firms are tied for first place as the best ways to get an interview. Thus, networking can play a major role in landing your dream job. Knowing people who can make the right introductions is a tremendous advantage. When it comes to getting your foot in the door, who you know can be as important as what you know. Of course, who you know is only a valuable asset if you're smart enough to make it work in your favor.

Frequently, key positions that cannot be filled from within are broadcast through informal channels. Even before a search firm is contacted or an ad hits the classifieds, word gets out that ABC Company has an opening. Oftentimes, through referrals and the right introductions, a job candidate lands a preferred position. Some call it luck, being in the right place at the right time. I prefer to think of it as *making things happen through networking*.

Networking starts long before you begin looking for a new opportunity. Successful people develop relationships with hundreds and even thousands of people during their careers. You build relationships with people you work with, including customers and vendors. You bond with people in trade associations and community organizations. What matters is that you have a network of friends and associates who will support you. I can think of no better time to use your network than when you're in the market for a career change.

Effective networking also includes headhunters. Always be cordial when they call. You never know what card life may deal you, so build your network as a safety net.

When you've decided to make a change, spread the word to your contacts. Let them know what's going on in your career. Don't start off by asking for a job. Instead, say that you are calling to get guidance and possibly a few names to call.

Don't limit your networking to business. Talk to people at your church or synagogue, country club, and civic organizations. Get out your high school and college yearbooks—look for names of old friends who are now movers and shakers. Go through your Rolodex: ask your friends and relatives to come up with names you might have overlooked. I know a man who networked for six months—he talked to 255 contacts, visiting at their offices and meeting them for breakfast, lunch, or dinner. He practically made a career out of networking. One contact led to another, and he finally found what he was looking for.

A source of networking that you may have overlooked is the interviewer who doesn't hire you. This individual can be a wonderful contact. As many hiring authorities have said to me, "Sometimes I really like a particular candidate, but her background just isn't right for the position. So I keep her in mind if anything else comes up. With her permission, I'll send her résumé to professional peers at other companies." Keep this in mind if you had great chemistry with the interviewer, but didn't receive a job offer.

40

What to Bring to an Interview

Start off with a positive attitude. Be well prepared and you'll come across as self-assured and confident. These are intangible things, but they are far more important than anything tangible. Of course, there are a few tangible items that will also help. You will absolutely need a fresh copy of your résumé, a reliable pen, and a notepad.

While all three are obvious, you'd be surprised how many candidates show up without them. Asking to borrow pencil or paper makes a negative impression on the hiring authority. Your notepad should already include prepared questions for you to ask—and it's okay to refer to your notes as often as you want.

Other things that I recommend you bring are addresses, phone numbers, job titles, and any other information you might need for completing a job application. This includes contact information for all references and previous employers. Be sure to have zip codes and fax numbers and e-mail addresses, if available. Not only does this save time, it shows you came well prepared.

Depending on your field, take a portfolio so you can show some of your top accomplishments. An architect might take drawings, an advertising executive might take ad copy, and an engineer might take blueprints. Some candidates have what I call a "brag book" containing copies of letters of recommendation, citations, and so forth. The opportunity may not present itself to use these tools, but it's better to have them with you than to wish you had brought them along!

41

Know How You Can Benefit the Company

A what's-in-it-for-me attitude is a sure way to repel the hiring authority. You should walk in filled with ideas about what you can do for the company.

All too often, candidates focus on their own needs. Their questions are self-centered. "I'd like to do my work at home. Do you have flex time? Would it hold me back if I'm not seen at the office? How fast can I expect my first promotion?"

Such subjects may be important to you, but they're poison during the early stages of an interview. You'll eventually find out what you want to know. Just don't push it. This is the time for you to convince the hiring authority that you have something of value to the company.

At MRI, we tell job candidates to think FAB—Features, Accomplishments, and Benefits. Basically, this means identifying a problem the company has and providing a solution based on your past success with a similar problem. Then, you summarize how it will benefit your future employer. You build a case on your value as an asset.

A newly hired person is always assessed through his or her potential contribution. You provide a service, and as such, are a commodity. The hiring authority must decide what potential is worth—in other words, your salary. Thinking of yourself as a commodity may seem impersonal, but it is a reasonable approach to seeking employment. Let's face it, business is business. What you're paid to do on the job must be justified on the other side of the ledger.

4 2

Rehearse!

Think of your interview as an actor thinks of a performance. What does an actor do before she performs? She rehearses! So much is riding on how you handle the interview—and you can be sure that other qualified candidates are "auditioning" for the same job. It's not enough that you have the best résumé going in. If you perform poorly, you may blow it. Don't think you can wing it during the interview. Believe me, nobody is that good.

Interviewing is not something you do frequently, so have your spouse or a friend play the role of the interviewer. List questions that you're likely to be asked and have your answers down pat. If nobody is available to role play with you, practice in front of a mirror. Repeat over and over what you want to articulate during the interview until you can say it with complete confidence and sincerity. Practice makes perfect. You might even consider videotaping yourself—this way you can fine tune your presentation until you feel comfortable and confident enough for the actual interview.

43

Are You
Committed?

Many people think about changing jobs for a variety of reasons. They aren't making enough money, they haven't advanced as quickly as they'd like, they don't get along with their boss or coworkers, and so on. In other words, their career is not perfect and they think they can do better elsewhere.

You may have some very good reasons to change jobs—but you must be sure it's what you really want to do. Changing jobs is a big step, and it doesn't always make life better. In fact, many people who make such changes wish they could have their old job back.

There's a lot at stake with a career change. There's always the risk that your next boss will be intolerable, the corporate culture will be a turn-off, you won't get along with your coworkers, and so on. Adjusting to a new work environment and unfamiliar surroundings is no piece of cake. It may even mean moving—which itself is a hassle. You'll be the new kid on the block and have to start all over. There's security in familiarity. Taking on a new job with a different company is a journey into the unknown.

Are you willing to take this risk with no guarantees of a change for the better? Are you convinced that it's what you want to do? If not, back off. There will be other candidates going for the job like hounds after a rabbit. If you're not completely committed, you'll be left in the dust.

4 4

Does Your Family
Support You?

Okay, you're committed to making a career change. But does your family share your commitment? It's essential to get your children, your spouse, or your significant other involved in the decision. You're not doing this by yourself. Their future rests on what you do.

If you're part of a double-income family, you have to consider your spouse's career before accepting an out-of-town job offer. If your spouse earns as much as or more than you do, this complicates matters. In any case, the two of you had better make sure you're on the same wavelength. You don't want to end up where one of you will have an unreasonable commute—or, worse, end up living apart during the week, as some couples are forced to do. You must think about what's best for both of your careers. Making a move that benefits one career but hurts the other is tantamount to taking one step forward and two steps back. If your move isn't right, the damage to one can end up hurting you both.

Let's say you're a one-career family, or your career is top priority and your change is agreeable to your spouse. This doesn't necessarily eliminate his or her anxiety. You must communicate with your partner, making sure he or she can be an informed participant in the decision-making process. Otherwise, you may find yourself meeting a lot of resistance—without your spouse behind you, you're in for some tough sledding.

Your career change involves more than financial considerations. The quality of life can greatly fluctuate based on where and how often you relocate in the name of upward mobility. A wife whose job is rearing children will want a comfortable neighborhood. You must both be content with new schools and opportunities to enrich your children's lives. As you're adjusting to your new job, most of the responsibilities of new home ownership will rest on her shoulders. She'll have to reconstruct her own network—from sitters to carpools. It will take lots of time to find the best grocery, dry cleaners, pediatrician, and so on. These changes can be distressing—especially if your family is happy where it is.

A move may also mean leaving extended family and close friends. Do you want your children to live where they have no cousins, aunts, uncles, or grandparents? What about your own parents and in-laws? What happens when they're elderly and require your care-taking? It's never an easy job, but even tougher when you're hundreds of miles away.

4 5

Landing a Job Is a Full-Time Job

If you're presently employed, just skim this for future reference. This message is directed to anyone currently out of work and anxious to land the right job. Read carefully.

I recommend that you approach your search with the same vim and vigor as you would a job you love. Put in a full day—eight hours or more of productive effort. Set your alarm clock for 7:00 a.m. and go through your normal workday morning routine. Instead of heading out the door, head for your desk or your table. Here at your home office, you send out résumés, make phone calls, take notes on all your conversations, search the Internet, place follow-up phone calls, network, set up interviews, and, in short, go full-speed ahead with your search. Can you see what will happen? Instead of sitting around feeling sorry for yourself, you're working. You're making something happen. You're staying on top of things. You're in control.

You're reading books and articles on job hunting, you're gathering information, and you're in daily contact with the people who you believe can help your cause. You're constantly networking—meeting your contacts throughout the week. By taking control of your destiny, you build self-confidence and self-respect—two vital elements to take to interviews.

You want to have many interviews. Why? Because you can accomplish only so much by staying at home. You have to go out and see people. The more interviews you do, the better you'll handle them. And the more exposure you get, the greater your chances of landing a dream job. It's a numbers game. You can't hit a home run when you sit on the bench! Get up to bat enough times and everything will fall into place.

4 6

Last-Minute Preparations

Okay, you have an interview tomorrow morning, and you've done your homework. Now you're thinking, "What have I missed?"

Be sure to confirm your appointment. This goes beyond etiquette. It's your chance to ask an all-important question: "What's tomorrow's agenda?" You can find out exactly who you're meeting, her position and function, and perhaps even the kinds of questions she's going to ask. If you're working with a search firm, the headhunter will fill you in, so don't make this call—unless he suggests it. But if you're on your own, make the call.

Find out how much time has been allotted for your interview and if you're going to be interviewed by more than one person. If so, find out how much time you'll have between interviews. It's okay to ask if there's anything you should be prepared for in advance. The more you can find out before the interview, the better it will be for everyone.

Make sure you are packed and ready to go with pen, paper, résumé, and portfolio or brag book. Make sure you have directions to the inter-view site—and allow an extra half hour for travel. If possible, make a dry run. Tricky traffic patterns or construction could result in a delay.

Make sure your clothing is well pressed, your shoes are shined, and your hair is neatly trimmed. Go through one more rehearsal the night before, and get a good night's sleep.

Tomorrow is an important day. Good luck.

The Interview

*I'm often asked to rate the importance of the
job interview on a scale of 1 to 10. I give it a 10.
For the record, I believe everything is riding on
how well you do during the interview process.
No matter how good you are, if you interview
poorly, your chances of receiving a job offer are
almost nil. The job interview is the moment
of truth.*

47

All Eyes
Are Watching You

From the moment you head out your door for an interview, pretend that a hidden camera is following you. It's recording everything you do, and the tape will be sent to the hiring authority. Maintain this mindset until your interview is over.

Why? Because you never know who's watching. Granted, it's unlikely that you'll cut someone off in traffic who turns out to be the interviewer. Or you'll treat a waitress in an impolite, unpleasant manner, and a company executive at a nearby table sees the entire incident. But I've lost count of the candidates who washed out because they behaved improperly when they thought nobody was watching.

One day while a candidate waited in a reception area, a young bearded man with long hair sat down beside him. The young man attempted conversation, but the candidate ignored him.

"Whatcha here for?" asked the young man.

The candidate turned his head.

"What's the matter, man, the cat got your tongue?"

"It's none of your business why I'm here," the candidate snapped.

During the interview, the candidate was startled to see the young man walk in and say to the hiring authority, "I'm sorry to interrupt . . ."

"That's okay," the recruiter replied. Turning to the candidate, he said, "I'd like to introduce you to my son, Brian."

The candidate turned several shades of red. Needless to say, he never made the first cut.

A few years back, a candidate was flown to the west coast for an interview. The company paid for his lodging at a luxury hotel. During his stay, several towels disappeared from the candidate's room. The interview went well, but the hotel manager reported the stolen towels to the company. The hiring authority told us later that it was the reason why the candidate lost the job.

Behaving with integrity costs you nothing. Be polite to everyone— receptionists, secretaries, even the janitor. Being rude or dishonest can cost you plenty.

48

What to Wear

I don't agree with the expression, "Don't judge a book by its cover." Book publishers know people do judge books by their covers and, consequently, go to great lengths and expense to design them. Similarly, the clothes you wear are your cover, and hiring authorities will judge you by them.

Good grooming is always a plus. All things being equal, the odds favor a job going to an attractive candidate. There is only so much you can do to change your facial features short of plastic surgery. But clean, shiny hair neatly trimmed and styled can enhance your appearance. Men should pay particular attention to facial hair—beards, mustaches, and eyebrows shouldn't be overlooked. Nor should ears and nostrils! Women should avoid heavy or dramatic makeup—go for the "daytime" look. Either gender can benefit from a consultation with an image stylist.

How you dress tells a hiring authority a lot more about you than how your facial features happen to be arranged. Your clothes reveal who you are. If you dress too casually, it suggests that you used poor judgment preparing for the interview. For example, a candidate interviewing with an investment banking firm wearing a loud sports jacket and an open shirt collar is sending several messages, none of which helps his cause. At worst, he shows disrespect to the established customs of the banking industry.

I purposely selected investment banking to illustrate my point because of this particular industry's stodgy reputation. Remember the adage, "When in Rome, do as the Romans do." Many companies embrace a dress code where golf shirts and khakis are perfectly acceptable. Still, don't wear such attire to an interview unless the headhunter or the hiring authority suggests it.

As a rule of thumb, wear what is stylish and tasteful. Make sure your clothes are well pressed and wrinkle-free. It's important to have a crisp look. Men should wear a dark suit—navy, black, or gray—with a white shirt and a tie that complements the suit. Shoes should be in good condition, well shined and preferably black. Socks should match the suit, and the tops should not show when you sit. Limit your jewelry to a good watch, a wedding band, or a college ring.

Women should also stick to suits. Skirts should reach the top of the knees; trousers should be generously tailored. Again, dark colors are best, but lighter neutrals such as tan or beige are acceptable. Hosiery should match either your skin or your shoes. Blouses must fit properly. If you can't keep your underwear from showing, wear something else. Wear little or no fragrance. Dangling earrings, clunky jewelry, bangles that clatter or jingle are a no-no.

The goal for both men and women is to appear serious and professional.

It's important to remember that standards of dress will vary based on geography, climate, and industry. Shorter skirts and Hawaiian shirts are popular business wear in some venues. What it boils down to is doing your homework so you can mirror the appropriate dress code.

A popular axiom at MRI is: "Dress for where you want to be, not where you are." This means dressing at least one level above what the position might actually require. As a general rule, it's always better to err on the side of dressing up than dressing down.

One last tip: Even if your interview is scheduled on the company's "casual day," don't dress down. There's ample opportunity to observe the custom once you're hired.

4 9

First Impressions

You only get one chance to make a first impression. In an interview, it had better be a good one. With other candidates competing for the position, a poor first impression can knock you out of contention.

Here are eight tips that will help you make a good first impression:

1. *Be readily available.* Busy executives will ask to interview you after hours or even on a weekend. By accommodating them, you demonstrate that a minor inconvenience won't interfere with your desire to get the job.

2. *Arrive on time.* Show up late for an interview and you can kiss the job goodbye.

3. *Carry an attaché case.* This makes you look professional and well organized—both are positive traits.

4. *Greet the hiring authority with a firm handshake and a friendly smile.* A limp handshake has eliminated otherwise qualified candidates. You should also extend a firm handshake to women. Otherwise, you will leave the same wimpy impression with them as you will with men.

5. *Make eye contact.* In western culture, failing to look people in the eye is interpreted as having something to hide. It gives the impression of being dishonest. At the very least, it implies you have little confidence and low self-esteem.

6. *Extend common courtesy to everyone.* Behave as if everyone from the receptionist to the hiring authority's colleagues are observing you. You never know who will say what to whom after you leave.

7. *Walk briskly.* It gives the impression of purpose and intent. People who shuffle appear to lack direction and have an idle mind.

8. *Minimize small talk.* It's okay to chat briefly after an introduction, but this is not the time for spinning yarns. Get down to business quickly. This shows you are serious and have respect for the hiring authority's time (as well as your own).

50

Be Prudent with Expenses

When you're invited out of town at the company's expense, spend money as if it were your own. Generally, the company will send your airline tickets and arrange to be invoiced by the hotel for your lodging. Upon submitting your expenses, don't pad it with such things as snacks, tips, parking fees, or transportation.

If you dine at the most expensive restaurant, drink the most expensive wine, or treat a friend at the company's expense, that's exploitation. Overtipping and outrageous cab fares look highly suspicious. Believe me, you're not the first to take a cab from the airport—the company knows what the fare is—and doesn't like you taking it for a ride!

You can leave two very bad impressions with imprudent spending to and from an interview. First, you'll appear dishonest, or second, you'll appear foolish. Either way, you're getting yourself into some mighty hot water.

51

The .000111 Factor

During the average round of golf, the total time the club actually touches the ball is under one second. Isn't that amazing? With all the hours spent taking lessons and reading books, there's so little contact with the ball. This analogy represents the relatively little time spent in interviews compared to the number of hours worked as an employee.

Let's say the average person works a 40-hour week for 45 years, for a total of 90,000 hours. Our statistics reveal that this individual will average five jobs, and will average a little more than two hours of interviewing per job. Hence two hours of interviews produces 18,000 hours of employment—a ratio of 9000 work hours to one interview hour, or 0.000111 percent.

Viewed this way, it's a momentous hour, isn't it? Considering the impact on your life, it underscores the importance of a stellar performance during an interview. From a financial viewpoint, assume that a great interview lands you a superior position and increases your paycheck by as little as $4 an hour. You'll earn an additional $36,000 during your employment. Of course, with an extra $10 an hour, that's $90,000 in additional income.

Note that my figures don't include the extra earnings you'll receive if you are hired sooner as opposed to later because you interviewed poorly.

I like to use these numbers to emphasize what's at stake during an interview. You must do it well. The relatively little time you spend interviewing over the course of your lifetime can be your most lucrative hours ever.

5 2

Not All Interviewers Know How to Interview

Don't assume that all hiring authorities know how to conduct an interview. Not all people who hire employees are human resources professionals. Some interview so rarely that, quite frankly, they don't know what they're doing. A study taken a few years ago stated that the average executive interviews fewer than 12 hours a year. Not only are they not good at interviewing, they don't like to do it.

Just the same, they have the authority to hire you, and if you're the victim of a poorly conducted interview, your chances of getting the job are greatly diminished. You, the candidate, must make sure the interview goes well—and provides the interviewer with enough information to know you're the best for the job. Sometimes this means you must take charge.

There is a knack to doing this. You must be subtle. If you come across as aggressive, you'll irritate the interviewer. So, what if the interviewer doesn't ask you the right questions?

For starters, you can say something like, "I'm sure you've had a chance to look at my résumé, Mr. Jones, but I'd like to give you a few details." This statement opens up the door for you to strut your stuff.

Briefly describe different positions you've held and what you've done in them. He can take notes to review later while deciding who's the best candidate. By taking charge, you'll give him reasons to hire you that he wouldn't otherwise know. Meanwhile, if other candidates only answer what's asked, guess who has the best chance of getting an offer?

5 3

A 50–50 Chance

Statistics show that the odds are about even for a company to hire the right person for the job. This isn't necessarily the best candidate. Of a dozen people being considered, any of six could work out, but one of the other six is hired.

Hiring and relocating are expensive, but even more costly is putting a person in a position where he or she doesn't belong. Most companies are aware of this risk when they recruit, so it's no wonder that executives don't enjoy conducting interviews. They don't like being in a position where the chance of success is only 50–50.

I think you need to understand the mindset of the interviewer. People typically think it's the candidate who's apprehensive during an interview. The person across the desk is equally uncomfortable. He may be doing something he normally doesn't do. He probably has 20 projects all crying for the hour he's giving you. Furthermore, he's under pressure to match a person with a position and if he doesn't succeed, he has a serious problem! He wants this hour to be well spent, but the odds aren't in his favor. In business, unlike baseball, .500 isn't a good batting average.

5 4

Interviewers'
Recurring Nightmares

Put yourself in the shoes of the interviewer. It's her job to interview candidates until she's certain she has the right one. But how can she ever be sure who is the best person? And what if she hires the wrong one?

This is a big responsibility for two reasons. First, she has an obligation to the candidate. The interviewer understands how her poor decision can negatively impact the candidate's career. In addition to personal trauma, a short-term stint in a new job is a black eye on a résumé. It makes getting the next job more difficult. Second, the interviewer suffers a setback by bringing the wrong person on board. Not only is there the cost of turnover, but the wrong person in a key position can damage her entire team. Furthermore, turnover is bad for morale.

Most experienced executives have hired wrong people at some time, so they're very aware of the potential harm. The very nature of business is to take risk; however, when people's lives are affected, hiring and firing goes beyond day-to-day risk-taking. It's more personal. And it involves multiple relationships.

It's important for you to understand this aspect of your search. The more you understand the interviewer's perspective, the more effective you'll be in an interview. At the very least, by understanding her recurring nightmares, you'll feel comfortable knowing that she's a human being just like you.

55

A Two-Way Conversation

L et's look at an interview for what it is. It's two people discussing a business proposition. Certainly throughout your career you've had meetings that were similar to an interview. Not only did you survive them, you excelled.

An interview is simply a conversation. That's it. Two people discussing a common interest. With this concept in mind, you can function at peak performance. All too often I've seen talented people choke during an interview. What should have been a piece of cake was a nightmare because they had a distorted view of what was taking place. Instead of having a conversation, they assumed a role they thought was appropriate. They politely answered questions. For fear of appearing presumptuous, they remained passive throughout the entire interview. In their misguided effort to make a good impression, they came across as unassertive and dull! As an interviewer, what conclusion would you draw about such people?

Of course, the better you do your homework, the more at ease you'll be. Preparation not only builds confidence, it relaxes you. Think about successes at other meetings—remember how you dazzled them when you were well prepared. You oozed with self-confidence. And you didn't hesitate to express yourself because you knew your business. You earned the right to be heard. This is exactly how to present yourself in a proactive interview.

A word of caution: you can say too much during an interview. A woman once told me, "Most people think I'm harsh and stern. I suppose it's my facial expression. I get caught up in my work, and I won't allow myself to be distracted. I'm very direct and candid with people, and they misinterpret me."

She was trying to convince me that she was a good worker. I heard something else I didn't care for. She came across as overbearing and inflexible. She might have felt comfortable with herself, but I didn't think she'd be compatible with MRI workers, so I didn't hire her. In my opinion, she lacked people skills.

Other people derail themselves when their testimony contradicts their behavior. A candidate might say she's very thorough, but when the interviewer discovers she knows practically nothing about the company, he's probably not going to put much stock in anything else she says!

5 6

Silence Isn't a Flaw in the Conversation

A ll too often, candidates interpret a brief period of silence during an interview as a bad sign. They view silence as a flaw in the conversation. In an attempt to keep things going, their impulse is to break the silence. This can be a fatal mistake.

A temporary silence isn't a bad thing. On the contrary, it's very natural for people to pause when talking. Nonstop dialogue isn't necessary—don't feel uncomfortable when this happens during an interview. And don't feel obligated to speak when a silence occurs.

Now by no means should you refrain from speaking up when you have something to contribute. A hiring authority doesn't want to hog the conversation, plus she wants to find out more about you. For you to remain silent when it's your turn to speak is definitely a flaw in the conversation. Like I said, an interview is two way.

Just the same, don't feel pressured to talk when you have nothing worthwhile to say. Candidates can get into trouble by running off at the mouth.

5 7

Two Salespersons and Two Buyers

In every well-conducted interview, there are two sellers and two buyers. Both interviewer and interviewee wear the hats of vendor and customer—and throughout the interview, they switch hats back and forth.

When you walk into the hiring authority's office, you have a dual mission: To sell yourself as the right person for the job and to decide whether this is the right company for you. The interviewer's dual mission is to sell you on the company and to hire the right person for the job.

Too often, candidates approach interviews wearing only their salesperson's hat. They're constantly selling. Consequently, they appear anxious and sometimes overbearing. A person may be a wonderful candidate for the job, but comes on too strong, casting a shadow of doubt in the interviewer's mind. He thinks, "Why is she trying so hard to sell me? Is it possible nobody else wants her?"

Think about the times you encountered an overbearing salesperson. His aggressiveness was unpleasant. It's human nature to resist high-pressure sales because we don't like being pushed. It makes us uncomfortable. Overselling during an interview will provoke the same reaction.

During the course of the interview, you may be simultaneously selling and buying. How does this work? You may ask a good question that not only elicits information, it also projects to the interviewer a favorable impression. "What good insight," the hiring authority observes. Your question demonstrates that your thought processes are intelligent and logical.

As in other forms of negotiation, both sides buy and sell. In business situations involving a long-term relationship, both parties must part completely satisfied. Ideally, each thinks, "That's the best deal I ever made." This is also an ideal conclusion to an interview. Both interviewer and interviewee should be elated because each has filled a need.

5 8

Interview
the Interviewer

Since virtually every job requires communication skills, it's important that the interviewer understand that this is one of your strong suits. Asking pertinent questions makes the process more interesting by creating a positive tension that generates energy. Thought-provoking questions tell the interviewer you're alert and interested in what he has to say. If you don't ask questions, you leave these impressions:

- You think the job is unimportant or trivial.
- You're uncomfortable asserting yourself.
- You're not intelligent.
- You're easily intimidated.
- You're boring.

None of these impressions works in your favor. If you're uncertain you'll be able to think on your feet, come prepared with notes. For some, this is helpful because it allows them to concentrate on the dialogue without having to think ahead. There is nothing wrong with referring to notes. It says that you are interested, curious, and organized.

5 9

Ask Tough, Crucial Questions

Before sending a candidate to an interview, I prep her to ask many questions. "One main purpose of your meeting," I say, "is for you to totally understand what you need to know about this company so you can decide if this is where you should be."

Going in with this objective, you're looking for information: What are the company's goals? What does it expect from the new hire during the next six months? For the next 12 months and 24 months? These are general questions; you expand from there. You have every right to ask pertinent questions that will help you decide if this is where you would like to work. Not only do you have the right to ask tough, crucial questions, it's expected! Ask about any subject you believe is relevant to your future. You have too much at stake to do less.

Just the same, don't believe the adage, "There is no such thing as a dumb question." I've got news for you—there are dumb questions. They prove interviewees either haven't done their homework or weren't listening. Intelligent questions strongly indicate that a candidate is in tune with the interviewer.

Nonetheless, we all find that our focus wanders from time to time because we're too concerned about what we want to ask or say next. Especially when you're trying to make a favorable impression. When you find yourself in conversation that's difficult to follow, ask for clarification. And ask for it intelligently.

For instance, don't say, "Would you mind repeating what you just said about fluid power?" This question suggests you weren't listening, or worse, you're simply not with it.

Instead, try this: "You mentioned the importance of fluid power. Could you elaborate on this?" This subtle rewording requires more detail from the interviewer, and you won't appear to be asking for an instant replay.

If asked, "Do you have any questions?" never respond, "No, I think you covered everything." If your mind is a blank and you can't think of a single question, take out your notes. Check them off one by one, saying, "You covered this one, and that one, too. Yes, sir; you discussed this one, and you answered this one." This demonstrated that you did come prepared and gave the interview some serious thought.

Don't hesitate to ask about company culture. General questions could be:

"Who are the company's biggest competitors?"
"Who are the company stars, and how was their status determined?"
"How are executives addressed by their subordinates?"
"What can you tell me about the prevailing management style?"
"How does senior management react to feedback?"

These pleasant questions are suitable for any interview. Further into the interview process, you can tailor questions to the company culture by focusing on specific areas. For instance, where there has been a recent reorganization, you might ask for details. It's okay to find out where you might fit in or, for that matter, where you won't. A 35-year-old senior systems analyst wanted to know if his personality suited the company culture, so he asked, "What do you believe is needed to succeed with this company?"

The interviewer replied, "We have a demanding, stressful culture that rewards quick reaction and spontaneity." The analyst liked this answer and decided he and the company would be a good match.

Another candidate was seeking a position in a high-tech industry. She said, "I am looking for a company that uses the latest hardware and software. And continuing education must be available. What can I expect?"

This proactive question says two things: you are particular about your future employer and are committed to personal growth. Both are positive messages.

A middle-aged woman with two small children wanted a job where constant travel and endless "face time" weren't the norm. She was being interviewed for a senior position with a *Fortune 100* company.

After asking the correct questions, she concluded, "I wouldn't be required to travel overnight, but several day trips each week would mean I'd rarely be home for dinner with my kids. There also would be weekend retreats about once a month. I passed on the job. I want to see my kids grow up."

Notice that when tough questions are asked, you might not always get the answers you'd like. That's okay. You're better off getting the downside before you take a job. Being proactive isn't simply a technique for making a good impression. It also yields information crucial to your decision making.

You must learn what kinds of questions are offensive or belligerent. If you've read about a sexual harassment suit or a class action suit involving the company, I suggest you avoid the subject. Your curiosity may be admirable and your journalistic tendencies an asset. But you may also appear to be a gadfly, a nitpicker, or a troublemaker.

Similarly, if you're asked a question that's blatantly illegal—related to age, religion, etc.—don't make an issue of it. Your values will dictate your response or nonresponse. But maintaining a civil and gracious presence is imperative.

As a candidate, you should never ask some questions until after the first or second interview—and others should wait until after you receive an offer. Unless it's brought up by the interviewer, don't discuss compensation during the first interview. And until you're actually on the payroll, never ask things like, "What holidays does the company observe?" and, "Do employees get a day off for their birthdays?" Questions like this suggest to a hiring authority that your priorities may be slightly askew!

6 0

---

22 Smart Questions

Asking no questions causes an interview to flounder, but too many questions can be annoying. In no particular order, the following 22 smart questions were compiled by MRI search consultants. Be selective—you don't have to ask every one.

1. If you hired me, what would be my first assignment?
2. What is currently the most pressing business issue or problem for the company/your department?
3. In this position, what goals would you like to see accomplished in the first 60 days? In the first six months? In the first year? What obstacles or difficulties stand in the way of reaching these goals?
4. Would you please describe for me the actions of a person who previously achieved success in this position?
5. Would you please describe for me the actions of a person who previously performed poorly in this position?
6. Where will this company be in the next 5 to 10 years?
7. Where is this job heading during the next 5 to 10 years?
8. Assuming I do a good job for the company, where can I go from here?
9. What do you enjoy the most about this company?
10. What level of authority does this position carry?
11. What plans does the company have to increase business?
12. Would you please tell me about the people I will be working with?

13. Why is this opportunity available?

14. How long has this position been open?

15. How did you get to where you are in the company?

16. Other than yourself, who else is involved with the hiring process? Is it possible for me to meet with them today?

17. What makes this company better than the competition?

18. Where does this position fit within the overall organization?

19. I'm sure that by the end of the day, I will have additional questions. Is there a convenient time during the next few days when I could call you?

20. When do you expect to fill this position?

21. What is the next step in filling this position?

22. Is there anything else that I could explain to give you a clear understanding of my qualifications and suitability for this position?

Later on—definitely not in the first interview and preferably after you have received an offer—you can ask questions such as (1) What are the employee benefits? (2) How much travel is involved? (3) Would relocation be necessary now or in the future?

6 1

Be Focused

One of my favorite movie scenes was in *City Slickers* starring Billy Crystal and Jack Palance.

On a modern-day cattle drive, Crystal's city slicker character asked the stoic cowboy Palance, "What is the meaning of life?"

After thinking for a while, Palance held up his right index finger and said, "One thing."

The Crystal character waited for an explanation, but that was it. There was a long silence.

"That's it? One thing?" the city boy exclaimed.

That was it. Not another word was spoken for the rest of the scene.

There is a lot of truth in this answer. Over the years, I have discovered that people who focus on one thing do well in this world. Remember this when you go to an interview. Remember the main reason you're there: to get a job. It's so easy to get sidetracked.

Too often during an interview, topics come up that are tempting—favorite subjects ranging from your children to your golf game—but more than a passing comment is inappropriate. Even when the interviewer asks directly about these subjects, avoid embellishing. You will waste precious time, and you'll create an impression that you aren't focused.

We've all been around people who appear to have a mission. Their focus is obvious, and with it they radiate self-assuredness. This wonderful quality comes across during an interview and creates a strong, positive impression. Hiring authorities also understand how it comes across to customers and coworkers. Such focused people are programmed for success, and they assure everyone that they will achieve it.

6 2

Lighten Up!

Interviewing for a job is serious business—particularly when you're seeking a position that you would die for! Just the same, don't feel as if your life depends on how you answer every question. Don't imagine that a single slip-up will have dire consequences.

In Section I, I emphasized the importance of preparation. Doing your homework builds self-confidence. You know what to expect and how to handle an occasional curve. Assuming you're well-prepared, there's no reason whatsoever to feel pressured.

One way to relieve anxiety is to arrive a few minutes early. Think positive thoughts. Walk in saying to yourself: "I'm going to meet a person who knows a lot about my industry. This will be an informative and fun experience."

Most importantly, act naturally and let the real you surface. If you come across as wooden or overrehearsed, the qualities that your friends and coworkers see in you won't shine. Furthermore, unless you lighten up, you come across as stodgy.

The more at ease you are, the more comfortable the interviewer will be. And it is important that the hiring authority like you. If you get the job, it's likely she'll be spending a lot of time with you.

Granted, getting an offer is serious. Just the same, don't approach the interview as if your entire career depends on it. Instead, think in terms of what you can provide a future employer and why the hiring authority should be excited about having you join the team. Put things in perspective. With the right attitude, you'll do just fine—so lighten up and go with the flow.

6 3

A Sense of Humor

I'm often asked if humor is advantageous in an interview. Personally, I can't think of many situations when it's not, so I'm all for it. A sense of humor is a wonderful asset in the workplace, and I like to think of ways to allow it to surface.

Hiring authorities welcome humor because it demonstrates that you keep work in proper perspective. When you can see the lighter side of a serious problem, you are able to approach it more clearly. After all, most difficulties are not as forbidding as they first appear, so it's good to let the interviewer see this side of your personality. Besides, humor can be a good antidote to stress. When people laugh, certain physiological changes take place that medical experts claim are beneficial—so it should ease tension in the workplace. A light comment at the beginning of an important meeting tends to relax people. Sometimes this is just the right touch to use with an irate customer or coworker. Of course, most of us like working with people who enjoy humor. They don't take themselves too seriously, and they're enjoyable company. Then too, a keen sense of humor is synonymous with wit—and wit is born of intelligence. No wonder hiring authorities look for candidates with this quality.

While a sense of humor is valuable, I must inject a few words of caution. There's a thin line between amusing and offensive. If you think there's the slightest chance you'll offend someone, keep quiet. Be particularly careful about saying anything that's politically incorrect. You may comment in jest, but it may fall flat with the interviewer. Don't risk insulting someone—no laugh is worth taking that chance.

Do not start your interview with a joke. I've watched too many candidates shoot themselves in the foot with the line, "A funny thing happened on the way to the interview . . ." Furthermore, even if the interviewer tells a joke that reminds you of another, keep it to yourself. One candidate got into a contest, matching joke for joke with the hiring authority. He couldn't resist reciting his complete repertoire of Monica Lewinsky–Bill Clinton jokes. He lost his bid for the job.

6 4

The Right Chemistry

We've all heard about people who meet, hit it off and become the best of buddies. They attribute their instant rapport with having "the right chemistry." When a candidate has the right chemistry with a hiring authority, most people chalk it up to good luck.

"If it doesn't exist between you and the interviewer, there's nothing you can do," they say.

I disagree. Fortunately, there are specific things you can do to create the right chemistry. I am so certain about this I routinely recommend three compliments to candidates. They are so effective, hiring authorities invariably call to say, "There was such chemistry between so-and-so and me that I plan to make him an offer."

Any candidate can use these compliments early in an interview to create the right chemistry:

1. *Make a positive comment about the geography.* If you're going for an out-of-town interview, just as you research the company, research the city. Then, during the interview, you might say, "I am impressed that there are four outstanding universities in this area. Education is very important to my family, and my husband has been wanting to enroll in some graduate courses." Another comment might be: "My wife's family is here, and I have two brothers here. Boy are we excited about moving here." If you live in the same area as the company, you can say, "We've lived here all our lives and just love it. I'm so glad my kids have a big extended family to grow up in. Plus we've been able to help our parents as they get on."

   No hiring authority wants to hire somebody who ultimately

wants to move three states away. Praise is taken as a personal compliment.

2. *Say good things about the company.* Look for positive things to say during the interview about the company. All too often candidates remain silent on the subject. Some even criticize, as if to prove that they did their homework or they're not afraid of confrontation. Frankly, anyone who fails to express sincere compliments is using poor judgment.

   A candidate might pick up in her research or during the interview that General Motors and Ford are company customers. "I see that you sell to GM and Ford," she might say. "I know how hard it is to do business with them. I know one company that's been trying to get its foot in the door for 12 years. I'm impressed."

   One candidate on a plant tour said, "If I hadn't seen this place, I'd never have believed it was a chemical plant. There are absolutely no odors." This candidate scored a lot of points with his remark, especially because on orders from OSHA, the company had spent 18 months getting rid of vapors.

3. *Praise the company's product or service.* Never forget it's the company's products and services that pay the salaries. Hiring authorities are extremely concerned with the quality the company achieves. So comment on how impressed you are. You have a choice of giving well-deserved praise, or keeping your remarks to yourself.

   Finally, you can always say something praiseworthy about the company's performance. Perhaps the company went from $800 million to $2 billion in five years. Or they had 100 percent employee participation in the United Way. There are all sorts of opportunities to extend a gracious compliment.

A word of caution: never be insincere. If you don't really mean it, then don't say it. Quite candidly, if you can't find something good to say, go home. After all, how hard is it to find something nice to say about a city, a company, or a product?

65

Selling Trust

When it's all said and done, what you sell in an interview is trust. People want to hire a person who will get the job done. They're buying performance. Consider the person sitting across the table. What's running through her mind? Two things: (1) Is this person who he pretends to be? (2) Can he do what he says he can do? If you can convince the hiring authority that the answer is an unqualified yes, you become a heads-up favorite.

One tragic mistake made by many candidates is exaggerating on their résumés. It comes back to haunt them during the interview. For starters, you can expect the interviewer will thoroughly read your résumé, and you can expect questions about it. So don't create doubt by overstating your experience. It's better to come prepared to discuss a particular shortcoming. This way you'll have credibility. Getting caught even in the smallest lie can terminate your chances of getting an offer.

Use common sense. You don't have to tell everything about yourself. In some instances, if no one asks, you need not tell. For example, if nobody mentions the three-month gap between jobs in the mid-1980s when you were in rehab, let sleeping dogs lie.

66

Know When to Shut Up

There's a tendency for candidates to keep mum for fear that they may disclose confidential information. As a consequence, they omit their accomplishments and the role they played in their company's success. They do themselves a disservice by excluding important facts that hiring authorities need to know.

Keeping confidences about current or past employers is certainly admirable, and you may be bound by certain legal and moral obligations not to reveal specific data. At the same time, you must divulge enough about previous experiences to convince the hiring authority that you are the right candidate for the job. Carefully think this through beforehand, so you feel comfortable about what you can and cannot say. Either way, saying too much or too little can work against you.

If you reveal privileged, classified information, the interviewer will conclude that you can't be trusted. When in doubt, explain the confidential nature of specific knowledge you possess. Properly stated, you will win the interviewer's respect.

6 7

The Proactive Interview

The days are long gone when candidates sat passively while hiring authorities drilled them. Today the interviewer is generally the person behind the desk. Otherwise, a casual observer might have difficulty telling them apart. Today's candidates are no longer passive. They are proactive.

In the late 1990s, the demand for good employees began to exceed the supply. This caused significant shifts in America's hiring processes. One notable change is that the interviewer no longer calls all the shots. Our boom economy will not continue forever, but I believe the current shortage of candidates will impact the interview process well into the twenty-first century. Both sides will benefit: with more autonomy, the interviewee will be more assertive and selective. This will result in a better match of human resources, thereby serving everyone's best interest.

Kudos to corporate America for adjusting to this fast-changing job market. Today's hiring authorities favor open dialogue, which promotes a broader exchange of ideas.

Unless you made a search in the late 1990s and are again seeking another position, you probably haven't witnessed this evolution. At MRI, we advise candidates to take control of their interviews. I am delighted to report that the results have been spectacular. Rave reviews pour in from candidates as well as our client companies. By instructing candidates to be proactive during interviews, our placements are running at a record high.

This assertive approach serves both the hiring authority looking for an ideal candidate and the candidate looking for the ideal employer. When both achieve their objectives, it's a win-win situation.

Typically, when an interview goes astray, it's because too little information has been exchanged—the fault can usually be shared. Unfortunately, it doesn't matter who's at fault if you don't get an offer that you want.

Simply put, being proactive means taking the bull by the horns. Let's say a hiring authority doesn't say much after glancing at your résumé. You must speak out. "Let me see if I can make things clearer by explaining the kinds of things that I've done."

This opens the door for you to present yourself in the most favorable light. You vividly tell of your past accomplishments.

Perhaps you rank in the top two percent of your company's top salespeople. A passive candidate would let his résumé speak for itself. But if you're proactive, you'll elaborate: "Two years ago, I was determined to open a lot of new accounts. I called on 10 new accounts each week while serving my existing accounts. I gave them the same high level of service they always received, and I didn't lose a single one. I also asked each one to recommend anyone who they thought would appreciate such service. Consequently, 55 percent of my new business was referred by present customers, and last year, I set the record for new accounts."

As you can see, it's one thing to simply make a statement, and quite another to explain. You can't just say, for instance, "I'm good with Excel." Instead, you must give a detailed description about what you did with Excel that benefited your company.

In summary, a proactive candidate doesn't simply answer a question and wait for the next one. She must determine what the interviewer should know about her so a sound hiring decision can be made. If the interviewer doesn't ask the right questions, a proactive candidate steers the interview toward the "right" answers, the ones that illustrate her most important strengths.

68

Opinion-Based versus Behavior-Based Interviewing

To excel at proactive interviewing, you must understand the difference between opinion-based and behavior-based interviewing. Each is a means of asking and answering questions.

When an *opinion-based* question is asked, it calls for an answer consisting of generalities. For instance, an interviewer says, "Your résumé has an 18-month gap between Brown Machinery and Black Manufacturing. Is this correct?"

"That's right," replies the candidate. "I did some consulting during that period."

If the candidate's answer is acceptable, the interviewer asks another question.

A *behavior-based* question necessitates a more detailed answer. Here, the candidate replies, "I worked for Brown for 12 years. When I left, I was eager to take some graduate courses. I attended classes 12 hours a week, taking three finance courses and getting my MBA. I also did some consulting with ABC-Point Company and XYZ Company. Let me tell you about an interesting program I installed for XYZ that increased their revenues by 15 percent . . ." The interviewer may ask follow-up questions to elicit more detail.

Similarly, a behavior-based response tells a story about specific accomplishments with explicit particulars, including anecdotal material.

Behavioral-based interviewing also addresses a specific situation, which can be a particular problem within the hiring company. The interviewer may say, "Can you tell me about how you handled a customer who was dissatisfied with your company's service?" A follow-up question may be, "What did you do to rectify the problem?"

If the interviewer does not ask for specifics, the behavior-based interviewee volunteers information as if the questions were asked. She says, "I'd like to tell you what I did for an unhappy customer," and describes in detail how she was able to handle the situation.

During the past several years, MRI has documented the results of opinion-based and behavior-based interviews. Our records indicate that under 50 percent of opinion-based interviews yield a good hire, as compared to over 70 percent with behavior-based interviews. When MRI uncovered these statistics, we started coaching both clients and candidates on the art of effective behavior-based interviewing.

Most hiring authorities are not proficient interviewers, so most of the questions you'll be asked will be opinion-based. However, as a skillful interviewee, you can still respond with a behavior-based answer. For instance, your résumé may state that you headed a cost-reduction drive that saved $900,000 in three years. The hiring authority may gloss over this and comment, "I see you saved a lot of money for your company."

An opinion-based response would be, "Yes, there were actually six different cost-saving programs I managed."

"Really?" the interviewer says, and changes the subject.

A behavior-based response would be, "Yes, I managed six different cost-saving programs. Let me tell you about one of them." You would give specific details so the interviewer has a clear idea about your talents, including what you can do for her company.

Prior to the interview, find out the hiring authority's agenda. The more you know in advance, the more you can customize your responses to meet her needs. Investigate her first priority for the hired candidate. This enables you ultimately to elaborate on how you will tackle the challenge, in part by telling what you have done in the past, and what you will do for the hiring company.

69

Paint a Vivid Picture

Let's say someone asks you about Monday night's football game. You don't just give the final score—you give a blow-by-blow description of the game. Just saying, "The Packers won 22 to 21," isn't enough. You explain that the Packers were behind 21 to 14 with 45 seconds on the clock and no time-outs. You describe how they completed five quick passes, and with no time left on the scoreboard and all receivers covered, the quarterback ran 12 yards up the middle for a touchdown. Then the Packers went for a two-point conversion with a pass down the middle to the fullback. This creates exciting images that leave a lasting impression.

This is how you handle an interview. Be prudent with details; when the interviewer says, "Tell me about yourself," don't reply, "Well I was born in a small town in western Pennsylvania to parents who were hard-working, middle-class folk. I was the third of seven children . . ."

Nobody wants to go back that far. Instead, say, "Well, Charlie, as you can see from my résumé, I have 20 years' experience in chemical engineering. What in particular about my career would be of interest to you?"

Or even better, say, "Well, as you can see, I have 20 years' experience in chemical engineering . . ." and cite what you think is a major contribution made to a previous employer that could similarly benefit the hiring company.

Don't go off on a tangent. You will bore the interviewer to death. Avoid excessive and superficial details. Zero in on a subject of interest to the interviewer. If he doesn't suggest a particular topic, choose one for him. Be prepared to tell ministories of quantifiable accomplishments.

It's okay to bring props to help tell your story. I've seen everything from written articles to an actual piece of equipment designed. If you feel a little "show and tell" will enliven the picture you want to paint, by all means bring along whatever you think it takes.

In the search industry, real-life examples demonstrate that you've been there and done that! This elevates you above other candidates who offer only a hypothetical solution to a problem. Your vivid picture proves you walk the walk.

It's especially effective when you mention people whom the interviewer knows. When you use real people and real examples, the story itself becomes real.

To the question: "How would you rate your performance?" you must avoid weakly replying, "Very good." More effective: "My boss rates us by profits, market share, and sales growth. In each of these areas I scored . . ."

Say you're asked to name your key accomplishments. A lame answer is, "I was responsible for managing 150 people." Far better is, "I managed a marketing department of 150 people, and we increased revenues by 25 percent over each of the past two years." Then, elaborate.

Don't speak in vague platitudes. Articulate clearly and specifically. It's meaningless to say, "I'm in management and have an MBA." Who cares? The interviewer wants to know what you do, what you're capable of doing day to day, week to week. Most candidates explain their qualifications by the seat of their pants. They think they know it so well they can wing it. Candidates who articulate precisely what they do are the ones who get offers.

See why details matter? It's the finer points that confirm you really know your stuff. Details give you credibility. So spice your story with details, and keep it interesting.

A Ph.D. in human resources whom I interviewed began by explaining a new process he introduced at his previous company. Then he said, "I probably made a fundamental mistake."

Up to that point I wasn't listening closely, but that phrase really caught my attention.

"I was anxious to get the job done," he explained. "Instead of involving all my people and getting grass-roots support, I tried to bulldoze the project launch so it could be installed by the end of the quarter. It was met with ho-hum acceptance. But I learned a valuable lesson. There are times when you must endure the frustration of the beginning stages in order to get your people involved. This way you get their input, and they buy into the program when you're ready to roll it out. People will support projects that they help to create. It gives them ownership. Boy, I never made that mistake again."

"Wow," I thought, "here's a man who admits a mistake during an interview." Most of all, however, I liked his story about why he involves people in the beginning stages of a project. Immediately, I knew he could apply this management technique at MRI, and I knew he was a perfect candidate for the opening we had.

See how you can create a lasting positive impression? Anything that paints a picture is so much more effective than talking in generalities. You articulate the message: "This is the problem I faced. This is how I dealt with it. Here are the results." And you tell it in living color.

By painting a vivid picture of what you have done in the past, you let the hiring authority know you can handle a similar situation in the new job. At the end of the day, isn't this the main objective of the interview?

70

Tell Them How Good You Are

There are times in everyone's life when one must toot one's own horn. An interview is one of those times.

I remind you again that you're selling a product—you. Tell a hiring authority how good you are. Don't let modesty get in your way. If you don't let the interviewer know what you are capable of doing, she might never know!

Oftentimes, candidates discuss their responsibilities in lieu of their actual accomplishments. Suppose the President of the United States walked into my office and I asked, "What do you do?"

"I'm head of the State Department, the Army, Navy, and Air Force," comes the reply. "The heads of Health, Education, and Welfare report to me. And the Interior Department . . ."

I'd say, "Wow, you have tens of millions of people reporting to you, and you've got this budget of trillions of dollars. I'm really impressed."

But then, I'd think, "Why was I so impressed? He just told me what his job was. I know he has a lot of responsibilities. But he never said anything that indicates he did his job well."

See where I'm going? Even the President must quantify how he performed. He must say, "I reduced the national debt from $700 billion to $100 billion. I did that in three years since taking office." Now that his accomplishments associated with his responsibilities have a time frame, I can see that he was good at his job. The same applies when you meet with a hiring authority. Don't just tell her what your job entailed—tell her how well you did it!

7 1

Learn about
the Company Culture

In Section I, I discussed how to investigate a company prior to an interview. Now let me tell you how to learn even more. You can actually begin picking up clues in the reception area. For starters, ask the receptionist what it's like working for the company. Be aware that she's observing you and the interviewer or her boss may ask her about you.

Keep your antennae up. Be attuned to what's going on around you. Here are a dozen observations that can give you some valuable insight:

- If you and other visitors wait for long periods, it's a sign of disrespect for the individual. This also applies if the receptionist leaves callers on extended hold.

- Look for plaques or posters that recognize and praise star performers. These indicate that the company appreciates its people.

- Look for company awards for industry leadership and active community citizenship.

- Are employees friendly—to you and to each other? Do people say hello and chat on the elevator and in the halls?

- Do workers appear to enjoy their work?

- Do managers treat subordinates with dignity?

- Do people look as though they use their time productively? Do they move about briskly or as if they have nothing to do?

- Do a few managers have large offices while many employees are confined to tiny cubicles?

- Do executives keep their office doors open or closed?

- Is the dress code formal or casual?

- Are facilities and furnishings in good repair? Stained carpet, peeling wallpaper and rickety furniture reflect bad times.

- Observe how managers interact with their subordinates when touring the company.

Once into the actual interview, you can listen for remarks and ask questions to gather more information about company culture. Consider the following 13:

- How is the interview conducted? Is dialogue formal or conversational?

- How does the company communicate to employees?

- How are decisions made? Top down or bottom up?

- Does the company encourage employees to learn more about the business?

- Is the company family dominated?

- Is there strong company philosophy that reflects the founder's values?

- When the family relinquishes the business, will these values be passed down?

- How are raises, bonuses, and promotions determined?

- What incentives does the company offer for exemplary performance?

- What are policies on flextime, staying home with sick children, bereavement, and so on?

- Is the company a good corporate citizen? Does it contribute both money and employee time toward civic activities?

- Is there a high turnover of people?

- Do all the hiring authorities ask the same questions? If so, this may be a sign that the culture is rigid and intolerant of individuality.

These may sound trivial, but they will reveal how the company treats its people.

If you sense tension, phrase your comments tactfully. "I've never seen such intensity in an office. Is this a busy period?" Don't imply negatives; indicate that you are simply trying to understand what you observed. During informal conversations with hiring authorities and other employees, ask questions about what they like most about their work and do they find time to have a life of their own. If the response is a rolling of eyes, laughter, or "It's the paycheck," it's a bad sign.

Many questions will be answered during the interview. I urge you to apply common sense when asking questions of this nature. For example, never ask about the company's policy on unexcused absences or tardiness. I suggest you focus on how the company treats its people.

72

Listen Carefully Before You Answer

Don't answer questions too quickly. Too often, candidates are so anxious to make a good impression, they fire off an answer before fully understanding the question. They think quick responses will imply that they're quick thinkers. But going into a lengthy treatise unrelated to the question does not impress anyone.

Listen carefully to what the hiring authority says, and wait until she's finished speaking. Interrupting is not only impolite, it could yield an inappropriate answer. To avoid interrupting, breathe in and out before speaking.

Remember, it's okay to ask the interviewer to repeat the question. This will buy you some time to come up with a good response. But do this judiciously. Too many requests for repeated questions will concern the interviewer.

If an important question stifles you, repeat the question in a way that requires the interviewer to restate it. For example, if you're asked, "What do you think is your biggest weakness?" you might respond, "I'm not sure I understand how to answer your question. Can you suggest the kind of weaknesses you mean?"

7 3

Respond Briefly

Proactive behavior-based responses will definitely impress the hiring authority. But it's important to understand that not every question requires a lengthy, drawn-out explanation. Sometimes, a brief response can be equally effective. Blow-by-blow descriptions aren't always required—and too much detail can make you appear dull, controlling, and self-centered.

Avoid getting off the track. Some candidates stray and talk about everything from their children to their golf game. When asked, "How are you?" don't feel obliged to tell about last week's flu and today's broken-down furnace. Stick to business-related subjects that showcase your job skills. This is what the hiring authority wants to hear.

Candidates who go into long, drawn-out explanations on everything are boring—and interviewers become gun-shy about asking additional pertinent questions. When the interviewer prequalifies a question with, "Can you briefly tell me . . ." that's your cue to chill out.

And if you have nothing worthwhile to say, don't bluff. Use one of my favorite lines: "I have a quick answer to your question. I don't know."

Finally, employers don't want new people who are marathon talkers. Such individuals are disruptive to coworkers.

7 4

Be a Good Listener

Good communication skills are essential during an interview. Unfortunately, most people think a good communicator is a person with excellent speaking skills. This is true to some extent, but speaking is only one part of effective communication. Listening is equally important. In fact, some people think being a good listener is the more valuable of the two skills. God gave us two ears and only one mouth, so perhaps we were meant to do twice as much listening as talking.

Obviously, you'll learn more when you listen than when you talk. In addition, listening is a sign of respect, good manners, and curiosity—all good qualities when you're in the market for a job. Contrary to what some think, you'll be more interesting if you listen rather than try to illustrate your sparkling wit. There's a lot you need to know about the company and the position—and you won't learn much if you don't listen.

Ask questions like, "What would you like me to accomplish short term and long term in this position?" You want to pick up key words and phrases that will tell you how to respond. Paraphrase some of the interviewer's expressions when you describe past accomplishments that relate to his needs.

These key words and phrases will vary. If you're in information systems, a phrase you may pick up is "working with users." So a response might be, "Approximately 50 percent of my job during the past three years has been working with users, determining their needs and providing solutions for them."

75

The Importance of Taking Good Notes

Throughout the years, hiring authorities have told me they didn't offer a job because a candidate didn't take notes during the interview. I've never been told someone wasn't hired because she took notes.

I've heard some interviewers frown on notetaking because it's distracting. Personally, I think the odds greatly favor the notetaker. Here are six reasons to take notes:

- It's flattering. It demonstrates you think what the interviewer is saying is important enough to write down.

- It's a sign of respect for the interviewer's time. By taking notes, you will avoid subjects that have already been covered.

- It provides you with a record of events. When you prepare a thank-you note afterwards, notes provide you with a logical progression. And you can quote the interviewer verbatim.

- If you have any questions later in the interview, you can refer to your notes. Remember, it's lethal not to have questions. While taking notes, you can jot down questions to ask later.

- It verifies that you are attentive. If you're taking notes, you're obviously listening to the interviewer.

- It makes you look conscientious. Did you ever notice most of the best students in school took copious notes?

15 Questions
You Should Be
Prepared to Answer

How you answer in an interview will determine any offers you receive. Weak answers can disqualify an otherwise qualified candidate. Likewise, strong answers will tip the scale in your favor.

It's not possible to know every conceivable question you'll be asked. But you can anticipate the most likely ones.

One way to prepare is to review your résumé and look for apparent "question marks" that jump off the page. Have answers, for instance, to explain wide gaps between dates of employment, a series of job changes within a relatively brief period, and new positions that seem horizontal or downward. To have a feel for what to expect, here are 15 typical questions with answers:

1. *What can you tell me about yourself?* Many hiring authorities ask this traditional question because they don't know how else to start the interview. Take advantage of it. Sell yourself and your qualifications right from the start. Give a short presentation on your professional qualifications and paint a vivid picture of one or two of your major achievements that you think will benefit the company.

2. *What is your ideal job?* To answer this question, decide what you are looking for. What did you like and dislike about previous jobs? What kind of environment suits you best? Do you need free rein or do you prefer close supervision? Review your strengths and be ready to express how they would make you a strong candidate for your dream job.

3. *Why should this company hire you?* Expect this question toward the end of an interview. You might want to review your notes before replying, and then say something like, "There are some definite challenges facing this company. I believe I have some unique experience that can help solve them. For instance . . ." Remember to speak in terms of what you can do for the company.

4. *Where do you picture yourself 5 to 10 years from now?* The best answer is a realistic one. If you say, "I see myself as CEO," you will appear frivolous. A proper answer is, "I believe through hard work and team effort, I can move into a key management position where I can best serve the company."

5. *How do you normally react to praise/criticism?* It's more difficult to say how you react to praise. You might say, "Frankly, like most people, I welcome praise, and it motivates me to work harder." When explaining how you react to criticism, say, "I welcome constructive criticism because I can learn from it. Besides, a long time ago, I realized I wasn't perfect . . ."

6. *What is one of your weaknesses?* The wrong answer is, "I don't have any." I recommend naming one or two that, in fact, could be interpreted as strengths. See Tip #79 for details.

7. *What is your opinion of the company you now work for?* Never knock a past or current employer. Try to focus on what you have learned and contributed.

8. *Are you considering other positions?* Be truthful. Don't go into details. If yes, simply say, "Yes."

9. *Do you consider yourself a highly competitive person?* This question is tough. You don't want to come across as ruthless. Still, you want the interviewer to know that you'll be an awesome player for the company. I recommend you structure your response in terms of how you can lead or support your team.

10. *Are you willing to relocate?* Be prepared to answer without

hesitation, "For the right opportunity, absolutely. What did you have in mind?"

11. *What motivates you?* "I'm at my best when I am challenged. And I want a position that will allow me to contribute to the company's growth. Hopefully, this company is where I will spend the rest of my career."

12. *What kinds of frustrations did you encounter with your last job?* Think carefully before replying. Every job has its share of frustrations. So talk about problems and obstacles you faced and how you overcame them.

13. *Do you consider yourself a success?* Answer in the affirmative by describing promotions, salary increases, and significant achievements that imply what you can do for the company. Remember to give behavior-based, vivid examples.

14. *What was the worst decision you ever made? How did you feel about it?* Be truthful. Emphasize what you learned from the experience. And avoid speaking defensively—make no excuses. Humility is a worthy attribute. Just don't confuse it with self-effacement.

15. *What do you like best and least about the position we're trying to fill?* Explain what you like best. Then add, "What I don't like is that I can't start right this minute."

All these questions and others should be well considered in advance of an interview. Put them in writing, take them to the interview, and refer to them briefly, if necessary.

77

There *Are* Dumb Questions

All our lives we've heard, "There is no such thing as a dumb question."

Well, let me set the record straight—it's a myth. There is such a thing as a dumb question. Candidates ask them all the time, and it costs them dearly. Sometimes they do it to be controversial, or they have nothing else to say. Or they haven't done their homework and they go to interviews unprepared. Asking a question with an obvious answer is a dumb question. Either you haven't given it much thought, or you're baiting the interviewer. Candidates also ask dumb questions because they weren't listening. Whatever the reason, it's unprofessional.

Avoid this by preparing a few good questions in advance. Then take good notes during the interview, jotting down questions as you go. It's likely that late in the interview you'll hear: "Is there anything you'd like to ask?" So have a few questions to ask—just be sure they're not dumb ones!

7 8

15 No-Nos

Not only should you avoid dumb questions, you must not make dumb comments. Here are 15 interview killers:

1. "Is the weather always this bad?"
2. "In the good old days . . ." "Listen, son . . ." "The girls in the office . . ." "When I was your age . . ." or "When you get to be my age . . ."
3. Addressing the interviewer as "dear" or "honey."
4. Referring to grown women as "girls" or "gals," and grown men as "boys" or "guys."
5. "I didn't get much sleep last night."
6. Dropping names of people you know who work for the company, unless they are somehow involved in your interview process.
7. Asking about lunch.
8. Volunteering an explanation of why you lost your last job.
9. Explaining why you won't do well in the interview.
10. Spicing your comments with religion, politics, race, gender, age, or ethnic references.
11. "Can I be honest with you?" "Trust me," and "Now, this is the truth . . ." These imply that you're not always truthful.
12. Lording it over others because you went to a top private school or business school.
13. Introducing yourself or asking to be addressed as "doctor."
14. Blabbing confidential information about your present or past employer.
15. Discussing yourself without explaining how it can benefit the company.

79

Turn a Minus into a Plus

At some time you're likely to be asked directly about your weaknesses. If the hiring authority has reviewed your résumé and spent some time with you, he's probably picked up on a few. Don't be alarmed, we all have our share of shortcomings. If asked to explain a weakness, don't deny it—that's the worst thing you can do. Prepare yourself to talk about a weakness in a positive way.

Let's say the hiring authority asks: "What do you think are your weaknesses?" Be careful. This question can be interpreted as: "Give me a reason not to hire you."

You certainly don't want to disqualify yourself. One answer is: "I hate to lose." Give an answer that is direct and honest, which makes your weakness a strength. Another example: "I'm very enthusiastic, and it's not always appreciated by those who don't express their emotions." You might confess, "I have a tendency to be so focused on my work, I forget to take lunch. I'm working on pacing myself." Or you might say: "I push my people pretty hard if a job is getting close to a deadline."

Consider a salesperson who is competing with several other candidates for a sales management position. She is the only candidate without management experience. When asked to explain this apparent disadvantage, she replies, "Throughout my career, I've been a top salesperson. I've had my share of good and bad sales managers. I think like a salesperson. I've been there, done that. I know exactly what qualities are needed in a sales manager. I know how I want to be treated, and I know what motivates me. I feel confident I can excel in sales management because the sales force will see me as one of them. I don't talk the walk. I walk the walk."

If something on your résumé or in your past stands out as a big minus, admit it and say, "It was an awful mistake, but I am a much better person because I learned so much from it."

Top executives understand that the only people who don't make mistakes are those who are afraid to take risks. Admission of failure is a sign of strength. It takes a strong person to say, "I was wrong." A smart person will also explain how she benefited from the experience.

80

Be Open to New Ideas

Nothing is constant but change. In the twenty-first century, things happen at an accelerated pace. Yesteryear's five-year plan has shrunk to 18 months. Change is not a way of life, it *is* life.

Anyone unwilling or unable to change is doomed to fall by the wayside. No company wants a candidate who resists new ideas. Every hiring authority worth his or her salt carefully assesses every candidate's ability to accept change.

When you join a new company, change will be necessary because no two companies or two jobs are alike. You'll have a different company culture, different coworkers, different management philosophies, and a different work environment. If you come across as inflexible, you'll be passed over.

Comments such as "I'm a professional," "I'm an achiever," and "I'm all for change," are idle ones. You must give behavior-based explanations of how you initiated change in past endeavors. Be sure to explain how the organization benefited.

8 1

Don't Bulletproof Yourself

None of us is perfect. If you appear flawless, you'll provoke the hiring authority to look for something that you'd rather not have surface. Again, you can describe a weakness that could actually benefit the hiring company.

It's okay to admit you're excited. It's expected. Otherwise you're disinterested or sedated. Avoid extremes in behavior—don't get manic and don't become catatonic. But don't be afraid to allow your personality to show.

82

The Job Is
Most Important to You

L et's face it, if you're between jobs, you've got more riding on the
interview than anyone. No matter what the outcome, the interviewer is going to work the next morning. He may be looking at a dozen
or more candidates. He can survive without you, but you can't survive
without a job.

Maybe you're absolutely the best person for the job. But if you don't
communicate this to the hiring authority, somebody else will be hired.
The interviewer will never know he made the wrong choice.

Even when you do get the job, you're only one of many employees.
Put things in perceptive. You may play a valuable role in the company,
but you're not the company's savior.

Since you have the most riding on the interview, you must take the
bull by the horns. I wouldn't let my fate rest on the whim of someone
else. I'd do my best to make things happen.

Your focus should always be on how you can contribute to the
company. Never speak in terms of why the job is so important to you—
desperation is repugnant to most hiring authorities. Avoid statements
like, "I really need this job," or "I'm a single mother with two boys . . ."

The interviewer may be a compassionate person, but she's not going
hire you to solve your personal problems. As far as she's concerned,
every candidate needs the job. Her interest is in what you can do for
the company.

83

Avoid Confrontation

One would assume every candidate has enough common sense to avoid confrontation during an interview. But based on the comments we hear, this is not the case.

No matter how tempting, never argue with a hiring authority. It can only be a no-win situation. Some interviewers will purposely provoke you to see how you react to superiors, subordinates, and customers. It may be a test—if you appear thin-skinned, it says you're insecure and can't handle not getting your way. Don't fall for this trap. Belligerence will only work against you.

Granted, there may be a situation when you can't let something slide. Matters of principle should never be compromised. Choose your words carefully, and above all else, avoid hostility. You have nothing to gain by challenging the interviewer on an antifeminist or racist comment. This would be a rare incident—one that is highly unlikely during an interview. Don't go into an interview with a chip on your shoulder.

It sometimes happens that a hiring authority will ask an improper or illegal question, one that would reveal your age or religious beliefs. If she asks, "When did you get your bachelor's degree?" it's easy to calculate how old you are, assuming you went to college right after high school. You're within your legal rights if you refuse to answer. You may risk losing an offer as a consequence. That is a choice you will have to make.

Avoid controversial subjects that could be viewed as antagonistic and malicious. In an attempt to show how current they are, some candidates will ask about negative media reports. For example, a candidate might ask, "What can you tell me about the class action suit on racial discrimination the company is facing?" It's not smart to confront hiring authorities with such questions.

Regardless of how well you feel you got along with the hiring authority, if you don't get an offer, don't call to ask why. It's okay to write to express your gratitude for the opportunity, adding that you would appreciate advice on how you may have interviewed better. Be sure to explain that you want to perform better on future interviews. In general, a friendly, well-written letter of this nature will generate a response.

8 4

Sell Yourself

Nobody can sell you like you can. You're the one who can tell your story with conviction and enthusiasm. Others may talk about these qualities, but only you can show that they really exist.

The hiring company is buying your services. So it expects certain performance in return. During the interview, you must convince the hiring authority you're worth the cost.

When two qualified candidates compete for a position, and one fails to sell himself, which one do you think gets the offer? Throughout my career, I've seen less qualified candidates land the job because they convinced the hiring authority they were winners. Never underestimate the value in selling yourself. You do this by:

1. *Coming prepared.* Like a professional salesperson does his homework in advance, so must you research the company and anticipate questions you'll be asked.

2. *Asking intelligent questions.* When you come prepared, you can ask smart questions and proactively participate in the interview.

3. *Listening carefully.* Great salespeople are great listeners who are interested in the customer's problems—and by listening, they come up with solutions. Here too, you must listen.

4. *Showing enthusiasm.* Nothing is as contagious as enthusiasm.

5. *Staying relaxed.* Sit back and enjoy the interview.

85

Don't Oversell!

U nless you're a skilled salesperson, it may be difficult to recognize the thin line between effective selling and overselling.

You don't want to come across as a braggart. Nor do you want to appear overly anxious or desperate. Subtlety is the key when broadcasting how wonderful you are.

Naturally the interviewer expects you to sell him on your qualifications and what you can do for his company. Don't disappoint him. But remain low key. A soft sell is much more effective than a hard sell. Nobody likes to be pressured into making a decision. It makes them feel uncomfortable. People resist such tactics. It builds a barrier between buyer and seller. Obviously, you don't want to build a barrier between you and the hiring authority.

On a final note, once the sale is made, shut up. Many clients have told me: "Joe was terrific during the interview, and I was going to make him an offer. But he kept pushing and pushing, and frankly, he talked himself out of the job. He simply doesn't know when to shut up!"

Another client told me about a woman who said too much after the interview. She was applying for a CFO position and remarked that she didn't like details. Every job has details!

86

The Advantage of Winning the Nobel Prize

Have you won a Nobel Prize lately? If you have, your reputation will precede you. There's nothing I can tell you about interviewing that will really matter. You don't have to be proactive, give behavior-based answers, or paint a vivid picture about your accomplishments. Nor do you have to worry about the competition, unless you're up against another Nobel Prize winner.

If you haven't won a Nobel Prize, I advise you to read this book thoroughly. It could have a tremendous impact on your career.

Fire in the Belly

Time and again, our clients tell us, "Find me somebody who has fire in the belly." When a position attracts lots of highly qualified people, this quality sets a particular candidate apart from the herd.

What is fire in the belly? It's the energy you generate that makes people excited to be in your presence. It's the passion you have for work and life itself. Your enthusiasm spreads like wildfire to everyone around you. This fire comes from within. It's an inner quality you can't fake— and you have to feel it for others to notice it.

Hiring authorities like this quality because it drives an individual to work long, hard hours with passion. Their work is a labor of love. It has the opposite effect on those who dread work and find it stressful and draining.

Some people confuse fire in the belly with being demonstrative. They envision people jumping up and down with enthusiasm. That may be an outward sign of fire in the belly, but others show it differently. Some individuals are equally fired up but have a quiet intensity. Their focus is pure, and their actions speak for them. They are equally exciting to hiring authorities.

One of my clients actually conducts a "FITB test." He rates candidates according to fire in the belly. A high rating guarantees an offer regardless of a "technical match." A low rating disqualifies a candidate.

88

Building Rapport

Generally, you can build rapport during the first five minutes of an interview. Reread Tip #49 on first impressions. I reiterate the importance of starting off with a firm handshake; a warm, friendly greeting; and good eye contact.

Let the interviewer set the pace. If she wants to engage in small talk, go with the flow. If she wants to get down to brass tacks, follow suit. Forget about expressing admiration of the mounted sailfish or the signed lithograph.

More likely than not, a hiring authority's opening remark will be a nonbusiness comment. It may be a simple ice breaker. Or she may be assessing your people skills. It's okay to look at her photos and say, "Looks like you're a Little League mom, too. Last year my son and my daughter both went to the regionals."

A sincere personal compliment is always appreciated by the hiring authority. This says you are observant and gracious. Remark about his nice-looking tie, his beautiful view of the city, or simply how much you have looked forward to meeting him. While your mission is to get an offer, it lets him know you're flexible and comfortable in social situations. You may ultimately be required to orient new employees, entertain customers, or play host to various visitors to the company. It also demonstrates that you have good people skills, which everyone needs to get along with coworkers, supervisors, and customers.

I'm constantly told by hiring authorities: "She had all the qualifications we were looking for, except people skills."

Today's companies are looking for candidates who know how to actively listen, stimulate dialogue, and offer positive feedback. This helps establish rapport.

Showing a genuine interest in the company is also an effective way to build rapport. Have a few prepared comments, and be sure to listen for things that are deserving of a compliment. Whether it's "I am impressed that the company has grown 28 percent this past year," or "Everyone seems so friendly," hiring authorities are no different from everyone else. We all like to be complimented. People enjoy having you praise their company. They take it very personally because it affirms they are smart enough to be there. They also feel good about being part of a winning team!

It's interesting, but you never know what door you may open when you tell something about yourself. One candidate, for instance, was applying for a position as chief financial officer and was asked about his outside interests by the CEO.

"My wife and I were not blessed with children," he explained, "but our favorite extracurricular activity is doing volunteer work at the Special Olympic events for handicapped children. Both of us play active roles. We're also foster parents for special children."

As it turned out, the CEO had a grandson who was a special child, and consequently, the two men had instant rapport. By the end of the interview, an offer was extended.

89

If the Decision-Maker Loves You, Anything Is Possible

Some time ago, a study concluded that 60 percent of hiring decisions were based on quantitative evaluation, such as education, work experience, and achievements. The other 40 percent were based on subjective evaluation, or what we call "soft skills." Soft skills relate to communication, negotiation, assessment, intuition, and so on.

So, while quantitative matters carry more weight than subjective matters, 40 percent is substantial. It definitely influences all hiring decisions, particularly when two candidates are neck and neck for the job.

But if whoever has the last word loves you, anything is possible. At the end of the day, if the top dog thinks you're the greatest thing since sliced bread, it's not going to matter if another candidate is more qualified. He's going to offer you the job—and it's probable that nobody will try to talk him out of it. Oftentimes, top executives make decisions on gut feelings. If that gut feeling tells him to hire you, the job is yours.

Never forget that life is not always fair. The most qualified candidate does not automatically get the offer. This does not imply that the odds don't favor him, nor does it mean he won't get the job. What it does say is that you could be less qualified and win. In that scenario, life isn't fair to the other guy, because you lucked out! My message here is that you always have a chance if you can sell yourself better than other candidates.

9 0

Be Likable

If you haven't figured it out by now, here it is in black and white: be likable! You'd think this would be apparent, but when you look around, you realize how many people just don't get it. They are unfriendly, nasty, self-serving, self-righteous, and arrogant—if there is a congenial side to them, they're hiding it!

Some people are so accustomed to being unpleasant, they're not even aware how they come across during interviews. Their attitude says: "I'm not in a popularity contest. I expect to be paid for my good work. You don't have to like me."

Of course, being likable goes beyond a popularity contest. If you're not congenial, it will affect the morale of your coworkers and will determine your team skills. It's also a fact that people will go the extra mile for people they like.

How important is being likable in being tapped for your dream job? Consider this: one company has an unusual way to evaluate. It's called the "Is this somebody we'd like to have lunch with?" test. If a candidate is not someone you'd invite to lunch, the company passes on him. To me, this test makes perfectly good sense because it's important to like your coworkers.

91

Never Badmouth a Present or Past Employer

If you happen to work for the most miserable boss in the world, who's mistreated, underpaid, and taken complete advantage of you—don't breathe a word of it in an interview. It's a cardinal sin to criticize any employer. It's tantamount to biting the hand that feeds you. No matter how justified your feelings, it will communicate all kinds of negative messages. For one, it suggests you have a problem with authority. Second, it says you were incapable of moving out of a bad situation because you were lazy, stupid, timid, or not worth hiring elsewhere! Third, the hiring authority will wonder how long you'll wait before saying bad things about your new boss. Finally, you could even be viewed as a troublemaker. The interviewer will think, "There are two sides to every story." This is not the kind of doubt you want to create. It's too easy for him to put your file at the bottom of the stack and look for another candidate.

One candidate I sent to an interview had worked for "the worst of the worst bosses." His turnover of managers was off the charts. The candidate was so unhappy working for him, he chose to leave the company. Still, when asked during an interview why he had left, he replied, "I learned all I could from my boss, and it's time to move on so I can learn new things."

The hiring authority personally knew the candidate's boss. He admired the candidate so much for his diplomacy that an offer was made at the end of the interview.

9 2

Take Criticism Lightly

It happens occasionally that you may face some form of criticism on an interview. The reasons can run the gamut: you might simply draw an impolite interviewer, he could be testing you, and so on. Whatever the reason, accept criticism graciously. This means remaining calm and refusing to take offense.

A quick temper says you're insecure and can't take rejection. It also indicates you don't react well under pressure.

If a hiring authority asks why you've had three jobs in the past two years or your grade point average is much lower than he likes—stay cool. Don't offer excuses. If he points out that your productivity fell for two consecutive years at your previous job, simply explain you learned from the past. Elaborate on how your lessons make you a valuable employee for his company.

In the world of business, where risk is common, everyone will make mistakes sooner or later. Remember, it takes a strong person to admit a mistake.

9 3

Give Sincere Compliments

A sincere compliment is a good ice breaker when you first meet someone. But remember: the key word is "sincere," so don't say anything that you don't mean. It's not necessary to sparkle with charm. Gushy, insincere compliments will do more harm than good. Sometimes the sweetest words are the simplest:

"I am very pleased to meet you."

"I am happy to be here."

"I've been looking forward to talking with you."

"I'm grateful for this opportunity."

"I really admire this company. I'd love to work here."

94

Multiple Interviews

As a rule of thumb, the higher up the corporate ladder, the more interviews you can anticipate. Rarely is an offer made following a single interview.

Generally, a company will want several people to have a look at you. This way, the company can affirm its first impressions. It also enables you to evaluate the company more thoroughly.

Don't let down your guard, thinking a callback means you've got the job. Prepare for every interview as if it were the first. Review your notes, prepare good solid questions based on what you have observed. Tailor your inquiries to your next interviewer. For instance, you may begin with human resources, then go on to sales, marketing, perhaps even the CEO. Each person has a different agenda and different expectations of you. One manager may look for confidence, an affinity for figures, and a critical eye; another may value articulate speech, a knack for navigating spreadsheets, and a good memory, and so on.

Inquire about each person before the interview. If you're working with a headhunter, ask her. Or ask whoever first called or interviewed you. Find out the interviewer's position, the agenda for your next interview, what kind of information she wants, and how much time will be allocated.

Don't try to guess the agenda from a person's title. Not every marketing vice president or chief financial officer is a clone of others you have met. Jumping to conclusions can get you into a lot of trouble.

The fact that you're being interviewed for a particular position means there's a need somewhere. Or there are opportunities not being exploited. By asking the right questions and doing your homework, you should be able to discern those problems. Think of the interviewer with a load of bricks on her back—and you are the person who can remove some or all of them. So you must understand each person's agenda and give behavior-based explanations about how you will solve her problems.

It's possible that during the course of several interviews, one interviewer will be the designated "bad guy." He may jerk your chain just to see how you react to stress. Stay cool. Simply answer his questions and move on.

Serial interviews typically involve three to five meetings, but there can be more. Not every interviewer may have authority to hire you, but he or she may have a voice in the decision. And it's possible that a high-ranking executive may have the power to veto everyone with a final aye or nay. So stay true to your mission. Convince everyone that you are the ideal candidate for the job.

95

The Panel Interview

Now and then candidates are invited to interview with a group. Whether across a table or in a more casual setting, you're outnumbered. And guess who's the center of attention?

To prepare for a panel interview, ask some friends or family members to rehearse with you. Generally, you'll be told who's attending. Come prepared, take notes, listen carefully, and ask appropriate questions. Be proactive and give behavior-based answers. Just as you build rapport with one hiring authority, here you will do so with a small audience.

Trying to guess who's most important in the room and focusing on this person will get you into trouble, especially if you're wrong. The dominant personality is not necessarily the senior employee. Furthermore, you risk alienating the whole group. It's probable that the hiring decision will be made by consensus.

Establish eye contact with each person. Always focus on whoever is speaking. It's okay to glance around and gauge the behavior of the others, but remain attentive to your partner in the conversation.

Some dread panel interviews, preferring a one-on-one encounter. Hiring authorities know panel interviews are stressful and are typically empathetic. Note that when you get to this stage in the hiring process, it's a good sign. Why else would the company tie up so many key people?

96

Doing Lunch

There's a good chance you'll be invited to lunch, particularly if you're out of town or seeking an important job. This may be simply a measure of hospitality; nevertheless, remember where you are and why you're there. You're still a candidate, and what you say and do is being scrutinized.

Let your host set the pace. If she wants to avoid business while you break bread, follow her lead. If the conversation is an extension of the interview, act accordingly. If other managers join you, behave as if you're in a panel interview.

Even though your host may order a drink, I suggest you avoid alcohol. A single glass of wine is okay at an evening meal—but only if your host orders one first. Despite what you may think, there is nothing to be gained from a drink or two. There is a downside: alcoholic beverages dull your senses. If you think a drink is necessary to relax and heighten your sharpness, you may have a problem.

When it's time to order from the menu, ask your host to recommend something. This will help you set some parameters on cost. If your host orders without regard to price, then the choice is yours. However, if she is frugal, you should be, too.

Select something that's easy to eat. A whole lobster can be a hassle. Spaghetti, ribs, and fried chicken are messy. So are big, fat, juicy hamburgers. Be smart and select something that won't drip, splatter, or smear your face or hands. And rein in your appetite. If you are starving, drink water. It will fill you up and help you eat less.

Where people are health conscious, order a hearty salad for lunch. If you're in an area that's known for its cuisine, by all means try it. But no matter how much you'd love a Maine lobster when visiting Portland, forget about it at a business meal.

There's a story that Thomas Edison wouldn't hire someone who salted his food before tasting it. Perhaps Edison figured such a person jumped to conclusions, and wouldn't exercise proper care during experiments.

Here are 20 more restaurant tips:

1. Don't order as if it were your last meal.
2. Don't leave the table to greet friends.
3. Don't order something that you have never eaten. This is not the time to experiment. One candidate ordered steak tartar prepared well done!
4. Set cups and glasses where you will not spill them.
5. When there is a wide array of knives, forks, and spoons, start with the piece furthest from the plate.
6. Use your bread plate if you have one (it's the small one on the left).
7. Drink the water on your right.
8. When squeezing a lemon, cup your hands.
9. Never speak with food in your mouth.
10. Don't change your order.
11. Don't send your food back.
12. Avoid food with bones.
13. Never use a toothpick in public.
14. Never criticize the restaurant.
15. Don't pick up the tab, offer to pay it, or suggest going Dutch.
16. Thank your host for treating you to lunch.
17. Turn off your cellular telephone—unless you anticipate critical news.
18. Be pleasant and courteous to servers.
19. Focus on the people at your table.
20. Speak softly—voices carry.

97

Etiquette During an Interview

Here are 14 tips to follow in an interview:

1. Be punctual.

2. Dress appropriately.

3. Groom yourself thoroughly.

4. Shake hands firmly.

5. Stand when someone enters the room.

6. Look people in the eye when conversing.

7. Don't use first names without permission.

8. Don't smoke or chew gum—even if the interviewer does.

9. Never interrupt.

10. Avoid gossip.

11. Never swear or use slang.

12. When someone tells a joke, no matter if you think it's funny, laugh, or at least smile.

13. Express your gratitude for the interview at the beginning and again at the end.

14. Extend your best manners to every single human being you encounter.

98

Are You Communicating the Right Message?

Think before you speak. When candidates say something that they didn't mean, they hurt their chances of getting an offer.

During a panel interview, one woman said: "I am very focused. Sometimes this gives people the impression that I don't want to talk to them. They interpret my intensity as unfriendliness, but it's really a reflection of how focused I am."

One person on the panel decided she was rigid. Another thought it meant she lacked people skills.

A young man said to a hiring authority: "Most people think I'm harsh and stern because of my facial expressions. I act that way when I'm very busy and concentrating on my work."

This statement was interpreted to mean he didn't get along with people.

Still another woman was asked, "Tell me about a time when you had to stretch your personality to match it with a subordinate."

The woman replied, "I don't do that. I am who I am, and if people don't like that, it's their problem."

For a bright person, she clearly wasn't thinking. Perhaps she was simply reflecting a healthy self-esteem. But the hiring authority inferred that she wasn't willing to compromise.

None of these candidates was offered a job. Be careful what you say. Saying what you don't mean can cost you!

99

Be Flexible

It's okay to dream about the perfect job. In the real world, however, no such job exists. If jobs were perfect, there would be no search firms. People would keep the same job for their entire lives!

So if you're looking for a perfect job, come back to earth. If you don't, you'll find fault with every job you take and become very frustrated. You must be flexible and willing to compromise.

I advise you to make a list of all the characteristics of your ideal job. Let's say you put down a great boss, highly enjoyable work, great opportunity for advancement, and so on. Now, you decide which ones are "must haves," and which you can live without. If you can find 10 out of those 15 or so in one job, it's worth your consideration.

Talk to friends and business associates—have them take this same test. You'll be surprised how many highly satisfied people can adjust to less-than-perfect jobs and be very content with what they do. But if you won't compromise when you find a great job with a specific flaw, you had better prepare yourself for a lot of disappointment.

100

---

30 Common-Sense Things You Should Know about Interviewing

Somebody once said, "Nothing is more uncommon than common sense." Accordingly, here are 30 things I think common sense should dictate:

1. Leave for the interview with plenty of time to spare for the unexpected: traffic jam, car trouble, etc.

2. Never go to an interview with a full bladder.

3. Never chew gum, and obviously not tobacco.

4. Don't allow the job title to influence your decision.

5. Wear conservative business attire. If the venue is very casual, overdress slightly. (Men: wear a sport jacket and tie. Women: wear tailored separates.)

6. Never consider moving anywhere your family has no desire to live.

7. Never ask to use the hiring authority's phone.

8. Don't look at your watch.

9. Remove your sunglasses.

10. Maintain good eye contact but don't stare.

11. Listen intently, so you don't have to keep repeating, "I'm sorry, but could you say that again?"

12. Don't ask about perks.

13. Ask for the spelling of each interviewer's name and write it down.

14. Don't mention a salary range in your résumé or during an interview.

15. Don't tailor your personality in an attempt to charm the interviewer.

16. Remain silent about your personal problems.

17. Go to the interview unaccompanied.

18. Don't park at a meter or in a tow zone.

19. Don't drop names.

20. Schedule nothing around your interview that will create a time crunch.

21. Turn off your cell phone.

22. Keep your eyes off the interviewer's desk.

23. Don't handle anything, especially personal belongings.

24. Get a haircut and shave if you need one.

25. Avoid strong fragrances.

26. Never be sarcastic.

27. If required to drive others, perhaps to lunch, obey the law, exercise caution, and stay calm.

28. Never criticize anyone, especially an employer.

29. If asked to complete a form or application, fill in every space. Never write, "See résumé."

30. Don't linger. A long farewell is annoying.

1 0 1

Closing the Interview

As a proactive candidate, you should initiate closing the interview. Remember not all hiring authorities are good at interviewing, and even fewer are good at closing.

To use a selling analogy, a good merchant can ask for the order without offending the customer. You want to achieve four objectives at the close of the interview:

1. Make it clear that you want the job.
2. Set the stage for the next step.
3. Create a final good impression.
4. Get an actual offer.

You want to be strong without aggression, and you want to leave having direction. In other words, if you're a contender, you don't want to be put on hold. Of course, if it's the first interview, closing with an offer may not be possible. Protocol may call for additional interviews—but certainly, you should pursue objectives 1 through 3.

Note that it's important to communicate that you want the job. Don't take for granted that the interviewer will automatically assume this. In fact, some hiring authorities are reluctant to offer a job if there's any chance of refusal. Show your enthusiasm. "Mr. Jones, I want you to know that I would very much like to work for this company. I feel confident I'll be able to contribute a lot, and I promise that I won't let you down."

Many clients have told me that candidates conveying this message received offers when more qualified but less enthusiastic ones did not.

Here are 14 effective ways to close an interview:

1. "I feel comfortable with you and with the position we've discussed. How do you feel?"

2. "Do you have any concerns about my ability to do the job and fit in?" This is an important question because it shows humility and gives you both the opportunity to address and eliminate a potential problem.

3. "Can you extend an offer at this time? Or would you rather set up another meeting?"

4. "How do I compare to other candidates you have interviewed?"

5. "I have a lot of information, and everything I need to proceed to the next step. Is there anything else you need from me?"

6. "I'm ready to make a decision based on the information I have. Is there anything else you need to make an offer?"

7. "What's the next step?"

8. "When should I follow up with you? Would it be appropriate to call next week?" This ensures closure, if not that day, in the near future.

9. "Is there anything personally or professionally that you believe would prevent my being a solid contributor in this role?" If "no," you can assume that the next step is working out the hiring details. If "yes," then you are positioned to address the interviewer's skepticism and quell it.

10. "I am very impressed with what I've seen here. And I really look forward to accepting an offer from you."

11. "It has been an interesting discussion. I would very much like to pursue it further."

12. "I'm sure that when I think about today's conversation, additional questions will come to mind. Is there a convenient time during the next several days when I can call you to pose these questions?"

13. "Is there anything else that I can elaborate on so that you would have a better understanding of my qualifications and suitability for this position?"

14. "Mr. Employer, your search is over. You will not find anyone else who will do this job as well as I can. If I were you, I would cancel all of the other interviews and make me an offer."

Each of these 14 comments is a proactive close. Each has been field-tested and works. So pick one or two you like and go for it.

1 0 2

Creating a Sense of Urgency

If you want to push the interviewer for a decision, you can apply some subtle pressure by creating a sense of urgency. This technique is risky so proceed with caution. Do it when you're willing to roll the dice, either because you are comfortably employed or have another offer that looks equally promising.

These four closes put a little heat on the interviewer:

1. "I have other offers pending that afford me tremendous potential. But I like what I see here, and I know I'm the right person for you. If you agree, let's talk turkey."

2. "Is there anything I have said that indicates I'm not the perfect candidate for this job?"

3. "I am in final-stage interviews with other companies, but I like what I see here."

4. "My family is scheduled to move within a couple of weeks. What do we have to do to speed up the decision-making process?"

1 0 3

Don't Keep It a Secret

With all things equal, hiring authorities choose people who clearly want to work for the company. It is not always the best qualified candidate who gets the job, but the one with the best attitude.

One of my favorite closes is: "Bruce, I'm not going to keep it a secret. I really want this job, and I know I will be fantastic."

With three candidates in a dead heat, and with two who are blasé, you can bet that the enthusiastic third will get the offer. May I point out that you can have a quiet enthusiasm. You don't have to jump up and down and scream and shout. If you really want the job, it will show, if you let it. Just speak up and say how you feel.

104

An Important Question: *"When Will I Hear from You?"*

Never leave an interview wondering what happens next. That's a bad place for a candidate to be! Ask the question: "When will I hear from you?" Don't accept a noncommittal answer. This is crucial information, so you must get a clear answer.

"We'll get back to you" is not clear. If you don't get a definite date, come back with, "If I haven't heard from you by Friday, may I call?"

If he vacillates, add, "Would you prefer that I fax you a note asking for an update?"

If this is acceptable, be sure to get the fax number—and the interviewer's e-mail address as well.

Consider the probability that you won't get through with one call. Say this: "I know you're busy; is it okay to keep calling until we talk?" Be sure to add, "I know there is a thin line between persistence and being a pest, but I'm very interested in this job."

If the hiring authority has any interest in you, she's likely to praise your tenacity and your attempts to move forward.

At this point, you've made it easier to overcome a potential obstacle. In fact, when you do call, thank her for the opportunity to show how persistent and thorough you are!

1 0 5

Playing
Hard to Get

While it's important that the hiring authority witness your enthusiasm for the job, you mustn't appear too anxious. Desperation isn't pretty, and it's not a quality a promising candidate should have.

Subtlety is the key in walking this thin line of playing hard to get for a job you want. Obviously, this requires diplomacy and finesse. As an analogy, picture a life insurance agent who says, "Your medical history is questionable. Let's submit your application and keep our fingers crossed." Rather than wondering if he wants the policy, the prospect wonders if he can get it! It's equivalent to giving something and taking it away at the same time. It's not easy but it's doable, and when executed properly, very effective. You must let the interviewer know:

- You're the best candidate for the position.
- It's possible for the company to hire you.
- A quick decision must be made.

Here's a script to follow: "John, you have my attention. I like what you put on the table. I see opportunity and future value here. I am currently looking at other opportunities, but they don't seem to measure up to what you have. How can we move this along? I do have some responsibility to those other people."

1 0 6

Money Talk

Discussing salary is—at best—a delicate operation, but one that comes to pass sooner or later. I advise bringing it up later versus sooner.

Never volunteer your current salary. If asked directly, "How much do you make?" answer, "Why do you ask? Are you ready to make an offer? What do you have in mind?"

Or another answer could be: "I am being paid for a different job with a different company. My current salary cannot be compared to this position. It is not an 'apples to apples' comparison."

If you do reveal your income, always be truthful. A hiring authority can verify the figure, and fudging can cost you the job.

A hiring authority may also ask, "How much will it take for you to accept this position?" No other question gets candidates into more trouble than this one. Nine times out of ten, the candidate will come back with a specific number. Two things can happen: your number could be too high or it could be too low.

I suggest you say, "I am interested in working for a solid company that's going places. I want a challenging position with growth and advancement potential. It's important to me to be a member of a great team. You know what I am making, and I will consider a reasonable offer."

This answer doesn't box you in too high or too low. In addition, it reveals that you're not primarily motivated by money.

Stay away from the salary subject until an offer has been made. As a good salesperson reveals the price of the product only after the benefits are demonstrated, do likewise.

1 0 7

Analyzing the Interview

While everything is still fresh in your mind, review the interview. As soon as possible, find a quiet place and jot down some notes. To get you started, address these eight questions:

1. *Whom did I meet?* Jot down brief descriptions of people you met, including names, titles, remarks, special interests, and a description so you can recognize them by name at your next meeting.

2. *What does the job include?* Be sure to describe the job, including what you like and dislike about it.

3. *What can I offer the company?* How are you uniquely qualified to make a difference? What do you bring to the table?

4. *What are the first things I can contribute?* List what you can do immediately for the company so you can discuss these points at a future interview.

5. *Where do we go from here?* Know what comes next in the hiring process so you can pursue the job.

6. *How did I make a good impression?* Know your strengths.

7. *Where did I slip up?* Record your missteps, not to punish yourself, but to improve your next performance.

8. *How can I polish my interviewing skills?* Mention briefly the moments when you felt uncomfortable or uncertain. These are areas that need a little more homework and review.

Remember, we learn from our mistakes. If you don't get an offer from this company, you have just prepared a study sheet to succeed another time.

The Postinterview

Your job search doesn't terminate at the end of the interview. Assuming all went well during the interview, there's still more to securing your dream job. This third section tells you how to get the job that's now yours to lose!

1 0 8

How to Use Your Headhunter *after* the Interview

So far, your headhunter has been instrumental in getting doors to open for you. He helped you put your best foot forward, but his work doesn't stop here. In fact, his services often prove most valuable after the interview. Indeed, his work isn't finished until you land your dream job.

Immediately following each interview, the first person you should contact is your headhunter. A good headhunter will want to talk to you as soon as possible. He'll want to hear your comments, get your perception of the company, the job, the chemistry between you and the hiring authority, and your concerns. He'll ask a lot of questions. Believe me, he'll want to know everything.

If you don't get an offer, he'll have the scoop on why you weren't hired. He'll have discussed you with the hiring authority. As intermediary, the headhunter can get both sides of the story. He'll be privy to feedback from the hiring authority that is rarely available to a candidate working alone. Depending on both parties' interests, the headhunter will arrange for the process to go forward or terminate.

When a misunderstanding occurs, the headhunter as go-between is invaluable. A hiring authority might have an invalid concern; upon discussing it with the headhunter, interest is rekindled. Otherwise a candidate might be written off. Likewise, a candidate might have concerns about the job that the headhunter can allay.

I can't tell you how many times we've had such situations at MRI.

After further discussions, an acceptable offer was made. Many of these placements resulted in years of success. Had the headhunter not stepped in, the two parties would never have gotten together.

As a third party, the headhunter can move things forward because she may know about the candidate's pending offers. By passing this on to the hiring authority, she can speed up a hiring decision that otherwise might have taken a longer time. Likewise, the headhunter can encourage the candidate by letting her know that someone else is in the running but dragging her feet. By promoting the hiring process, it's a win-win situation.

The headhunter can also serve as a mediator in negotiating a contract, bringing both sides to an amicable outcome.

109

The Postinterview Letter

Your thank-you letter to the interviewer should go out the day of the interview. Would you believe that 50 percent of all candidates fail to send a letter? This is not simply a courtesy. It's good business. It gives you a chance to pitch yourself as an asset to the organization. It showcases your communication skills if you take the time to craft a beautiful letter. And it reminds the interviewer that you're a class act.

Here are 10 tips on preparation. The postinterview letter should:

1. Be computer generated, not handwritten.

2. Be on your personal letterhead.

3. Express your gratitude for the interviewer's time.

4. State how much you enjoyed meeting her. "Thank you for sharing your thoughts on the direction of the company."

5. Verify your interest in the position, and emphasize that you are well qualified and confident you will do a great job.

6. Include something from your notes. This demonstrates your attentiveness.

7. Mention people that you met at the interview, if applicable.

8. Mention something that wasn't discussed at the interview, such as a special skill, a specific past experience pertinent to the new position, etc.

9. Contain no misspellings, no abbreviations, no poor grammar, and no inaccuracies.

10. Not be too flowery and limited to a single page.

I purposely do not include a sample letter here. Otherwise, multiple copies of it would start showing up in hiring authorities' mail. I want you to be creative and let your letter reflect your personality and the interviewer's.

110

More Money Talk

To many candidates, it seems smart to discuss money early in the interview process. "Why waste a lot of time only to find out that we're miles apart in salary?" they say. Wrong!

I repeat: unless the interviewer brings up the subject, stay away from money talk until an offer is made. With serial interviews, several meetings may occur before the subject is raised.

Remember the analogy of wearing both vendor's and buyer's hats? Before negotiations begin, put on your selling hat and listen carefully. A good salesperson hooks the customer before stating the cost. Have you ever asked a salesperson in the middle of a presentation, "How much?" What happened? Without missing a beat, she continued, "first let me tell you . . ."

If you're asked early on about salary expectations, a wise reply is, "Can we wait to discuss my salary? I would prefer to first explore opportunities and ways I can contribute to the company."

Generally, this will delay money talk. I can assure you odds of a bigger starting paycheck by discussing money later rather than sooner. Many hiring authorities have confided that they upped the ante as several interviews took place. On the other hand, I've never seen a company drop a salary figure. It simply doesn't hire the candidate!

Assuming you've held off salary discussions through the entire process, and an offer is made, it's finally time to talk turkey. Here are seven tips on discussing money:

1. *Know what you're worth.* Find out in advance what the going rate is for the job, so you have a figure in mind. You might discover you're worth more than you thought.

2. *Know what the job entails.* Be sure you know what you'll be doing before you accept a salary. You can't determine adequate compensation until you understand the job. Of course, if it's your ideal dream job, you might consider less money than a higher paying job where you won't be happy.

3. *Let your ambition and enthusiasm show.* Some candidates affect nonchalance when they should most strongly exhibit their zeal. Now's the time to release your fire in the belly.

4. *Make it known you're not driven strictly by money.* Don't give the impression you'd do anything for a buck.

5. *Let the company make the first offer.* If asked, "How much are you looking for?" come back with, "I'm sure the company will compensate me fairly. What does the company have in mind?" If it's too low, you have a place to start negotiating. If you ask for too much, you can price yourself out of the job.

6. *Find out the salary range the company is considering.* Another good response to "How much are you looking for?" is to say, "What range has been set?" Let the company show its hand first. The company may even offer more than you expected.

7. *Don't play cat and mouse.* Being too evasive can hurt your credibility. If asked a second time, state a range that you think will be adequate. Again, research your figures, and start high enough, but not too high.

111

Negotiating Your Salary

In general, candidates don't feel comfortable discussing money. For starters, they have little experience, so they'd rather leave it to the employer. This is dangerous and can be costly. Don't be naïve. The hiring company won't always act in your best interest when it comes to pay. You're negotiating with a profit-making company—and businesses watch their expenses. Good managers are always looking for ways to curtail costs, including salary caps.

Here are three myths about salary negotiations:

1. Quoted salary ranges are nonnegotiable.

2. If you try to negotiate your salary, it will insult a prospective employer.

3. Be willing to settle for less. It's easier to get a raise once you've proven yourself.

Don't fool yourself. Even the most benevolent employers want you for the fewest dollars possible. To determine what you're worth, check with friends and colleagues who work for other organizations. Read salary surveys in trade publications or on the Internet. Talk to former bosses, and best of all, if you have one, ask your headhunter! Then be prepared to negotiate. Don't be too quick to accept the first offer even if it's exactly what you want.

Depending upon the position you're seeking, a hiring authority may evaluate how well you negotiate your salary. If you're not prepared, you'll perform poorly. Chances are, the first offer is low and the hiring authority is prepared for a counteroffer. But if you accept substantially less than the going rate, the company might think something's wrong. Maybe you're not as good as you appear to be.

Think of a first offer as a starting point. The company wants you on board. This means you can ask for more. If you don't get it, you can agree to the original offer. You can always save face by asking about benefits and then say, "I am willing to accept this salary in light of your excellent benefits." Don't shortchange yourself by accepting the first offer and ending up at the bottom of the salary ladder.

Look at it this way: For a few minutes of discomfort during salary arbitration, you can increase your annual income by thousands of dollars. Isn't it foolish not to negotiate?

One important tip: Always state what you will do for the company to justify higher compensation. Do not give personal reasons such as, "I am on a tight budget," or "I have four kids in college." Your needs are not valid reasons for more money. If you can't live within your means, that's your problem.

I will conclude with the words of negotiation expert Chester Karass who says, "In business, you don't get what you deserve; you get what you negotiate."

112

Nonsalary Remuneration

It's possible to be paid less and earn more. This is why you must take a good, hard look at the entire compensation package. Of course, your base pay is important, but you must also determine what the extras are worth.

Throughout this book, I advise avoiding the subject of fringe benefits during the interview process. These are not issues that should influence your decision on where to work. However, they are a vital part of your compensation package, so once an offer is put on the table, it's time to discuss them.

Major fringe benefits include health and life insurance, relocation expenses, 401K and retirement plans, contributions toward stock purchase, signing bonuses, performance bonuses, and stock options. Others worth considering are day care, on-site fitness centers or exercise/recreation facilities, health club memberships, dining areas, and so on.

All these benefits and more have actual dollar value. You should include them in your compensation calculations. Depending on your age, health, and dependents, health insurance can be worth thousands of dollars over and above your annual salary. Check this by calling an insurance agent to learn what you'd pay if self-employed. Moving expenses can reach five figures. Bonuses considerably affect your net worth. And, of course, extras, such as health clubs, facilities, and day care, could cost you several hundred dollars a month if you typically use them.

Then there are stock options. This could be the most attractive part of your compensation package. They can be worth more than everything else combined. It's no wonder we read about CEOs who are paid one dollar a year in exchange for sizable stock options. These executives are willing to bet stock prices will rise significantly. Many other companies attract employees who agree to such compensation. Thousands of recent Silicon Valley millionaires can attest to the attractiveness of such a plan.

As you can see, the whole package can be worth a lot more than the base salary. So don't choke on the offer without learning about the extras.

Perhaps a situation exists wherein a hiring authority faces an internal equity issue. If you like everything else about the job, there are ways to negotiate around a low salary figure that enables her to work within her parameters, and you can get what you want, too. For instance, you ask for a guaranteed annual $10,000 bonus for the next three years. Plus you can get such goodies as a company car or a car allowance, professional membership dues, and a budget for professional development. This way, you and the hiring authority are both satisfied because you were willing to compromise.

1 1 3

Sleep on It

There's an Aesop's fable about Buridan's ass. It stood between two haystacks, unable to decide which was most desirable to eat, and starved to death!

When you are offered the job of your dreams, and terms of employment meet your expectations, it's perfectly reasonable to accept it on the spot. If you have reservations, however, ask for some time to make your decision.

It's okay to say, "This is a really important decision for me, and one that will affect my family. I'd like to discuss it with them. May I get back to you within 48 hours?" Any reasonable company will grant this request.

A word of advice: make your decision quickly—preferably before your head hits the pillow that night! If you procrastinate, the company may withdraw its offer. Nobody wants an employee who can't make decisions. Of course, you may also wish to talk to your headhunter, attorney, CPA, or a mentor. So you may even ask for three or four days before deciding. But if another candidate is waiting in the wings, you'd better decide quickly.

There is always the risk that while you sleep on it, the company will hire somebody else. Every headhunter knows a candidate who took too much time and someone else got the job. I remember one candidate who told a hiring authority, "It takes me two hours to drive home. I'll call you with my answer when I get there." When she made the call, she learned the position had already been filled!

On a final note, if you do decide to refuse an offer, notify the company. It's common courtesy. Furthermore, you may find an opportunity with this company another time, or the contact may prove vital to your network.

1 1 4

Other Job Offers

The hiring authority knows there may be other companies pursuing you. A little competition is a good thing.

But it may make your decision difficult. It's an enviable situation, but one you must handle with kid gloves. Ideally, it will create a bidding war between the two companies. If so, welcome it, but exercise extreme diplomacy or you'll lose in two ways.

You can only play this hand briefly, especially if other candidates exist. Since this is probable, tread lightly.

Let's say you're equally interested in both companies and company A makes an offer. Request a few days to think it over. Call company B to set up a meeting. Explain to the hiring authority that you have an offer from company A. Is company B in a position to match it?

Timing is crucial. If you've had serial interviews with company A, but are just getting started at company B, you're at a disadvantage. Sitting on an offer is risky business. If you prefer company B, you might have to stall company A. Just remember, a bird in the hand is worth two in the bush.

I have explained it's preferable to begin a search when you are already employed. It alleviates the pressure of such a scenario as this. It also makes a "slow no" much easier.

115

The "Slow No"

We've all experienced the "slow no." A prospect tells a salesperson, "I'll get back to you." Days and even weeks go by. Each time the salesperson calls, he hears, "I haven't made up my mind." Ultimately, the salesperson stops calling altogether.

When a company interviews candidates, it has a need to fill a specific position. Just the same, the company has other priorities. If the right candidate doesn't come along, there may be no urgency to hire anyone. And if you're not exactly what the company is looking for, you could get the slow no. I've seen candidates go through a series of interviews and end up on indefinite "hold." "When we make a decision, we will call you," they say. Just as candidates can be indecisive, so can hiring authorities!

As you can see, the slow no is far worse than an out-and-out no. You build up your hopes and are left hanging. You may even pass up your second choice and live to regret it!

You must be aware of how the slow no works. When you sense that it's happening to you—and, believe me, you'll know when it does—you must confront the hiring authority.

"Marilyn, last week you said the company would reach a decision. You know I am interested in the position. What's the decision?" Generally, when it gets to this point, the odds are against an affirmative reply. Just the same, there comes a time when you must fish or cut bait.

116

What If You Won the Lottery?

Would you take the job if you won the lottery? If the answer is yes, you're making the right decision.

I realize you have bills to pay and you have to think about the money. Just the same, don't take a job you know you won't enjoy, regardless of the money.

Consider other things besides the paycheck. Will you be excited when your eyes open every morning or will it quench the fire in your belly? Will you feel good about yourself at the end of the day? Will you feel most comfortable with the company culture? Will it allow you to be creative and offer you long-term opportunity?

Consider all of these issues before making your decision. You will eventually earn more money at a dream job with lower starting pay because you have a passion for your work. Most people perform better when they love what they do.

117

Coaching Your References

How well do you recall what you did on a job 15 years ago? Chances are the people you put down as references won't remember either. If you want high praise, refresh their memories. Otherwise they're not going to do you much good.

First, call to ask their permission: "I think XYZ Company has a lot of opportunity. May I use you as a reference?" Assuming it's okay, explain the positions you'll be seeking and add, "Please tell them anything you believe helped me succeed when I worked for you."

If you call a customer, say about the same thing with some minor modifications: "I'm thinking about making a change. I've enjoyed our wonderful relationship over the years. Would you be kind enough to talk to some people who may check me out?" Remind her how you handled her account and helped increase her turnover of inventory.

Your references will need to know what they're likely to be asked about you. I suggest sending them an annotated résumé, going over your achievements with them so they can articulate your strengths.

Obviously, employers expect you'll hand pick people who will speak highly of you. So why are they important to hiring authorities? Most are skilled at extracting information. They know what to listen for and how to read between the lines. You can bet they will check out your references, so choose wisely.

These eight tips will help you get the most mileage out of your references:

1. The best references are managers and customers. A satisfied customer is among the best references.

2. Choose a mentor who has followed your career and is rooting for you to succeed.

3. If your former company has a policy against giving references, ask the person if he'd extend a personal reference so he wouldn't be breaking a company rule, and take the call at home.

4. Ask your references to be open and honest. A good recruiter will pick up fibs or exaggeration, and this could be worse than no reference at all.

5. Some people can sell you better than others. If you select an introvert who can't express herself, she won't help your cause.

6. Letters of recommendation are worth their weight in gold.

7. Include a third-party business reference. This could be a contact from another department in the company, a vendor, and so on.

8. Allow a reference to express himself freely. Rehearsed scripts usually backfire.

1 1 8

Spend a Day in the Field

If you're applying for a sales or marketing position, ask to ride shotgun with a sales rep. Nothing beats sitting on the firing line. Most companies will accommodate you. It's better to find out now if you don't like the job. In addition, the company would rather not waste time training you. Makes good sense, doesn't it? After all, you'd test drive a car before buying it.

Generally, this advice applies across the board. You can ask to walk down the production line, visit information systems, graphic design, and so on. Meet the people you'll be working with—learn what they think about their jobs, their bosses, and the company!

You may also ask to attend meetings or conferences, or simply have lunch in the cafeteria to observe and talk with employees.

1 1 9

Restrictive Covenants

If you signed an employment agreement with your present employer, be sure to review it. It may contain a provision that restricts you from working for a competitor or limits what you can do. You may have signed a "trade secrets" or "confidentiality" agreement that could limit your activities. In recent years, some courts have restricted employees from working for another company, even if they didn't have an employment agreement.

These are limitations and restrictions you should know:

1. *Restrictive covenant.* This classic covenant prevents an employee from going to work for a competitor. In order to be enforceable, it usually has to be limited to a specific territory and be for a specific period of time. And those restrictions have to be reasonable. The specific territory may depend on where the employee worked. It could be a 50- to 100-mile radius, a county or state, or even adjoining states. The time period is often one to two years. If geographical and time limitations are too broad, the court may rule them unenforceable or modify them to a lesser area and timeframe. These limitations are to protect a former employer, not to restrict an individual from earning a living.

2. *Nonsolicitation restriction.* This prohibits an ex-employee from soliciting or wooing away the customers of a former employer. These restrictions usually don't have any territorial limit but may involve a period of time.

3. *Trade secrets and confidential information.* These are designed to protect information that belongs to a company against use by a competitor. Trade secrets might consist of technical information, formulas, pricing, customer lists, or other valuable information

that's not generally known. The information might be in documents, on a computer, or even in the memory of the employee.

4. *Doctrine of inevitable disclosure.* Circumstances exist in which a former employee has knowledge of trade secrets or other valuable information. It is possible for the court to conclude that, due to the nature of the new job, it is inevitable that the employee will disclose some or all trade secrets and information belonging to the former employer. The doctrine recognizes that a former employee may carry in his or her memory what is considered valuable proprietary information to a former employer's detriment. Such information is not limited to secret formulas; included are confidential marketing plans, blueprints, customer lists, and closely guarded management strategies.

The court may impose strong restrictions against any kind of disclosure, which can preclude the individual from going to work for a competitor. This can happen even when a noncompete agreement does not exist between an employee and a former employer.

The restrictions that apply to your changing jobs depend on your individual circumstances. If you feel part or all of the previous issues pertains to your present job, I recommend having a talk with your employer. You may be able to negotiate relief from some restrictions, especially if you have been a trusted employee. For example, by agreeing to stay away from key customers for a specific or permanent period of time, your employer may waive other restrictions.

If you think you may face a problem in this area, also discuss it with your new employer, who may be able to obtain legal advice for you. You might want to get advice from your own lawyer, even before talking to your current employer, because the applicable law and the attitude of the courts varies so much from state to state. The consequences for violating certain restrictions could be severe. A court could prohibit you from working for the new company, award damages against you, and assess up to triple damages for use of or obtaining trade secrets.

1 2 0

Review Your Plan Documents and Contracts

The adage that timing is everything certainly applies to changing jobs. You will want to be sure how the timing of your leaving will affect your rights to bonuses, stock options, and other benefits. Even if you don't have a formal agreement, you might have a letter agreement, describing such things as your compensation, bonuses, and commissions. Other provisions might be in an employee manual. Your pension rights under a "qualified" plan, such as a 401k, profit sharing, or pension plan, would be spelled out in the plan documents and in a summary plan description.

Timing could also have an impact on your obligations to your current company. Even if you don't have a formal employment agreement, you might have signed a letter in which you agreed to reimburse the company for relocation expenses, a recruitment fee, training, or a sign-on bonus if you jump ship too soon after the hire date, usually within one or two years.

For a long-term employee, many penalties have expired. But bad timing can cost you if you're on a vesting schedule for stock options or retirement benefits. You might also lose "trailing commissions." Since every situation differs, make sure you understand how much money is at stake by leaving immediately, as opposed to waiting until you are sufficiently vested. If you cannot calculate current values against vested values, talk with a certified public accountant. I've seen executives leave weeks too soon and forfeit vested proceeds in six and seven figures.

If you or a family dependent has a chronic health condition, the preexisting condition may not be covered with another insurance company. COBRA permits ex-employees to continue coverage for 18 months, but you must check into preexisting conditions' coverage in your new employer's health benefits. Certain terms of medical coverage can mean burdensome out-of-pocket expenses.

Also consider the time of year you leave your present company. A year-end bonus may be due. If you're entitled to a bonus that's one-third of your annual salary, you might want to stick around until it's paid before you give notice.

121

Leave on Good Terms

From a legal viewpoint, it pays to be honest. I strongly advise against lying to your employer before you leave to get additional compensation such as a bonus or commissions. Never deny that you have a new job—lay your cards on the table.

Don't compete unfairly with your ex-company. If you go after former customers, give away trade secrets, or knock your former employer, you'll risk legal confrontation that could be costly. The court may even force you to resign from your new job.

Of course the obvious reason to be loyal to the company you leave is because it employed you. If you worked there for any length of time, you have friends and coworkers still employed there—you owe loyalty to them. Finally, you want to maintain a reputation of integrity in your industry. Remember, you should never burn bridges.

By leaving on good terms, you'll win the respect of your new employer. You'll assure her that you're a quality person who plays by the rules.

122

A Blessing in Disguise

More than ever before, Americans are making midcareer changes. What was once considered a nightmare is turning out to be a rewarding, enjoyable experience. In today's mobile workforce, several careers during one's lifetime is the norm. So if you're on the verge of losing your job, or for that matter, you just feel burned out and want to do something different, there is no longer a stigma attached to changing jobs. Even if you're getting near retirement.

As always, the best time to plan a career change is before you quit your present job or are let go. This advice never changes! In the past, most people forced into midcareer changes did it with shame. It was seen as a sign of failure. In the new millennium, such changes are viewed as healthy and progressive. As the world changes, you must— welcome it at all stages of your life! Change is invigorating and exciting for everyone, regardless of age. Change is what keeps you young. Resisting change makes you seem old.

Americans in the prime of their lives today would have been considered elderly 25 years ago. Employers understand that people seeking midcareer changes are vibrant and, most important, have skills and experience that make them desirable employees. What's more, they have more working years ahead of them as the retirement age keeps increasing. A recent poll indicates that 75 percent of Americans said they plan to work past age 65, and 47 percent of retirees polled are still working. These Americans remember the phrase "retire and die," and they have no intention of doing that.

If you're thinking about a midcareer change, I wish you much success. I know with the proper attitude, you will thrive.

1 2 3

Brush Up on
Your Computer Skills

All experts agree: you must have computer skills. Without them, you're a Neanderthal. Older people see a computer as a word processing tool. They compare it to a typewriter, claiming, "It's for people who do clerical work." This kind of thinking dates you and makes you seem unwilling to learn new things. In truth, a computer is an incredible machine. It furnishes you with information that not only makes your work more interesting, it enables you to do it in less time.

The world is becoming increasingly dependent on computers and the Internet. You must have the necessary skills to use these invaluable tools. The number of Americans using computers at both home and work has doubled within the past five years, and approaches 50 percent of the total population. By 2010, home computers will be as common as TVs—and some experts predict, used more. Simple chores from personal banking to shopping will be handled on the Internet. Most high school seniors already log onto college web sites to check out curricula and enrollment procedures. They can even apply online. Those without computer skills will be deemed illiterate, especially in the world of commerce. As someone said, "Even a plumber who is not online will see his business go down the drain."

Whatever you do for a living, eventually computer skills will be mandatory. If you're thinking about changing jobs or are in the process, polish your computer skills. This may require a study course and some homework. It should be a wonderful learning experience.

1 2 4

A Balanced Life

All work and no play makes Jack a dull boy. It can also make Jack a dull executive. Employees must be well rounded, which means having balance in life. When you start a new job, remember that success at work must be in sync with your personal success.

If you spend too much time working at the expense of your family, you'll end up with personal problems that drain your productivity. Studies have shown that workers with unhappy personal lives are unable to focus. The stress of poor personal relationships creeps into the workplace. You cannot separate your work from your life—to be successful, you must succeed at both. Similarly, work problems go home with you. A person who is miserable at work will have difficulty being a good partner and parent. You are the same person on and off the job, so you must have harmony in both facets of your life.

Good balance also comes from community activity. No matter how busy you are, find time for a charitable or civic activity that benefits others.

A new job is a good opportunity to commit to a balanced life. Yes, a successful career is important, but it won't happen if you sacrifice your personal life.

1 2 5

Changing Priorities

A student once asked Albert Einstein, "Why are you giving the identical test we took last year?"

Einstein replied, "Because this year, all of the answers are different."

At different stages in your career, your priorities will change. If you're amidst a job change, this is a good time to think about priorities. Your skills have changed, your ambitions have changed, your family has changed. Your spouse may have a different job; your children are older, perhaps no longer dependent on you. In short, due to different circumstances in your life, you are a different person.

As you embark on a new career path, be sure to determine what is meaningful to you today. For instance, job satisfaction may be more important than a bigger paycheck. Perhaps you'd rather spend more time with your family and are no longer willing to take work home. Or, you may be inspired to make a difference in others' lives. Possibly, your financial responsibilities are greater and you're committed to work longer, harder hours. My point is: your life is constantly changing and so are your priorities.

Get your priorities right. Work is a means to provide for loved ones and have quality time with them. Find your comfort zone and realize that moving beyond causes anxiety and stress.

It's not an original thought, but if you need help with priorities, try, "God first, family second, and career third." I can't think of a way to improve on this, so it's yours to consider.

Notes

3. What If the Money Didn't Matter?

"... the desire to make more money should never be your primary motivation in a job search." Bill O. Jose, Woodbury, New York

"These six things are more important than getting more money ..." Bill O. Jose, Woodbury, New York

5. What Can You Uniquely Offer an Employer?

"If you're working with a headhunter, ask, 'What is the most important thing this company wants in a candidate?' " John Rosica, San Jose, California

"... assess your career to identify your greatest accomplishment." John Rosica, San Jose, California

"I am personally attracted to the candidate who shows passion for work." Bill O. Jose, Woodbury, New York

6. A Journal of Your Accomplishments

"... a journal of your accomplishments is also an impressive tool in an interview." John Rosica, San Jose, California

"... reviewing your journal is a great way to 'pump up' just before a job interview." Amy Cody-Quinn, Kona, Hawaii

8. Having a Game Plan

"During interviews, you will be judged by how well you articulate your goals as well as how you plan to achieve them." Bill O. Jose, Woodbury, New York

"A mechanical engineer had 12 years' experience in the refrigeration industry but didn't see a future with his employer." Bill O. Jose, Woodbury, New York

10. Don't Allow Rejection to Defeat You

"It hurts to be passed over, especially if you're unemployed." Cindy Lyness, Cedar Rapids, Iowa

"Rid yourself of all your negative thoughts and fill your mind with positive ones." Cindy Lyness, Cedar Rapids, Iowa

"It's personal," he said, "and I can't tell you more." Iacocca, Lee, *Iacocca, An Autobiography*, Bantam, New York, 1984, p. 127.

16. Research via the Internet

"To get started, find the company's web site." Dave Campeas and Patrick Sylvester, Philadelphia, Pennsylvania

"One excellent place ... is Hoovers.com." John Littman, Philadelphia, Pennsylvania

"Use search engines such as HOTBOT ..." Bud Jewell, West Palm Beach, Florida

17. What's the Company Culture?

"[Culture] is the biggest influence on how you'll fit in." Dave Campeas and Patrick Sylvester, Philadelphia, Pennsylvania

"Examine the Big Five accounting firms . . ." Dave Campeas and Patrick Sylvester, Philadelphia, Pennsylvania

". . . you'll spend most of your waking hours working at your new company." Dave Campeas and Patrick Sylvester, Philadelphia, Pennsylvania

". . . start with the library or the company's web page." Stacy Gulden, Winter Park, Florida

"Find out about a new leader's personality and style." Dave Campeas and Patrick Sylvester, Philadelphia, Pennsylvania

"Is the company a good corporate citizen?" Management Recruiters International Legal Department, Cleveland, Ohio

18. Talk to Present and Former Employees

"Here, too, you can search the Web for former employees." Bud Jewell, West Palm Beach, Florida

". . . consider going where company employees gather for lunch or happy hour." Bud Jewell, West Palm Beach, Florida

"Both former and current employees attend trade shows and association meetings." Bud Jewell, West Palm Beach, Florida

"There is nothing wrong with calling the receptionist to say, 'I'm coming in on Thursday . . .'" Tom Thrower, Oakland, California

". . . most managers will admire your assertiveness . . ." Tom Thrower, Oakland, California

20. Familiarize Yourself with the Product

"Nothing beats hands-on information about how the product works, or how it is made and sold." Bud Jewell, West Palm Beach, Florida

"Attend trade shows . . ." Bud Jewell, West Palm Beach, Florida

21. Check Out the Interviewer

"Just say, 'Hello, my name is . . .'" Tom Thrower, Oakland, California

"Is he a laid-back, casual type of person? . . ." John Littman, Philadelphia, Pennsylvania

"What's his background?" "How long has he been with the company?" Russ Hanson, Appleton, Wisconsin

". . . the majority of interviewers will admire your assertiveness." PJ Jones, Pittsburgh, Pennsylvania

22. Call the Interviewer

"The most direct way to find out what the interviewer is like is to call him." "Is there anything in particular that you would like me to prepare for tomorrow morning?" "Say, how long have you been with the company?" John Littman, Philadelphia, Pennsylvania

23. The Door Opener—Your Résumé

"... a well-written résumé should whet the appetite of the interviewer." Jeff Yeager, Lansing, Michigan

"... it's an appetizer, not a full-course meal." Edward Gridley, Lexington, Kentucky

"Make sure your résumé is printed from a computer." Lynn Stickel, Baltimore/Timonium, Maryland

"Tailor your résumé to what the interviewer is seeking." Dan Larson, Des Moines, Iowa

24. The Format of a Well-Written Résumé

"Make sure it passes the 20-second test ..." Edward Gridley, Lexington, Kentucky

"... margins between three-fourths of an inch to one inch ..." "Job-Hunting: Do's and Don'ts of Resume Writing," *CPA Client Bulletin*, April 1998.

"For legibility, break up text with headings ..." "Job-Hunting: Do's and Don'ts of Resume Writing," *CPA Client Bulletin*, April 1998.

"Break a series of thoughts into a list, such as career highlights, and use bullet points to indent them." Russ Melanson, Baltimore/Timonium, Maryland

"You shouldn't go back too far if you've held a lot of jobs ..." Jane Sanders, Baltimore/Timonium, Maryland

"Your résumé should be financial-driven." Edward Gridley, Lexington, Kentucky

"I don't like résumés that say, 'References upon request.'" PJ Jones, Pittsburgh, Pennsylvania

25. Résumé References

"I recommend listing six [references]. Two should be ..." Stacy Gulden, Winter Park, Florida

26. Proofreading Your Résumé

"A single typographical error or misspelled word can ruin an otherwise perfect résumé." Dan Larson, Des Moines, Iowa

"... spelling and grammatical errors tend to jump off the page." Russ Melanson, Baltimore/Timonium, Maryland

"It won't pick up on homonyms ... have someone with good writing skills review it." "Job-Hunting: Do's and Don'ts of Résumé Writing," *CPA Client Bulletin*, April 1998.

27. What to Do about Those Gaps in Your Résumé

"It's permissible to bury small gaps in your résumé." Karen Egan, Grass Valley, California

"Honesty is the best policy." Susan Young and Wayne Young, Morris County, New Jersey

"As an alternative to explaining a gap in the body of your résumé ..." Patrick Sylvester, Philadelphia, Pennsylvania

28. 11 Fatal Errors in a Résumé

"Avoid patterning your résumé after the same examples . . ." Jane Sanders, Baltimore, Maryland

"Hiring authorities are not impressed with . . ." Jane Sanders, Baltimore, Maryland

". . . a job objective limits the candidate. If the exact position isn't available . . ." Karen Egan, Grass Valley, California

29. The Résumé Cover Letter

"For this reason, many headhunters think a well-written cover letter . . ." Jeff Kaye, Dallas, Texas

"Don't get folksy or cutesy." Dave Campeas, Philadelphia, Pennsylvania

30. Why a Headhunter?

"Simply put, individuals currently working are more desirable to hiring authorities." John Littman, Philadelphia, Pennsylvania

"This means they have numerous contacts across the country." Patrick Sylvester, Philadelphia, Pennsylvania

"Most importantly, they have built relationships with their client companies over time." Susan Young and Wayne Young, Morris County, New Jersey

"Suddenly, a headhunter provides this individual with an immense job opportunity." Sam Sarafa, Ann Arbor, Michigan

31. Building Relationships with Headhunters *before* You Start Your Search

"Top headhunters are astute . . ." Ron Whitney, Elgin, Illinois

". . . I'm putting you in my database." Dick Kurz, Chicago (O'Hare), Illinois

". . . you wouldn't wait until April 15 to meet with an accountant." Ron Whitney, Sacramento, California

32. Why Headhunters Hunt Almost Exclusively for Employed Individuals

"People without jobs . . ." Russ Hanson, Appleton, Wisconsin

"First, an unemployed person is viewed as poorly organized." Ron Whitney, Sacramento, California

". . . he is making a major commitment." Ron Reeves, Elgin, Illinois

33. How to Sell Yourself to a Headhunter When You're Unemployed

"One reason is that an unemployed person is usually too aggressive . . ." Susan Young and Wayne Young, Morris County, New Jersey

They'll assume that if you're unemployed, you've already circulated your résumé and called lots of recruiters." Ron Whitney, Sacramento, California

"They like proactive candidates who help them with the research." Karen Egan, Grass Valley, California

35. Interviewing the Headhunter

". . . ask about his area of specialty. Find out how much he knows about your industry." Cy Tessin, Kalamazoo, Michigan

"Does your network go beyond your local geographical area?" Ron Whitney, Sacramento, California

"If you're unemployed, state exactly why. Be totally honest." Jeff Heath, New York, New York

36. Things You Never Say to a Headhunter

". . . nothing turns us off faster." Jeff Heath, New York, New York

37. How to Keep Your Search Discreet

"Companies want to hire experienced people . . ." John Littman, Philadelphia, Pennsylvania

"She will use due diligence . . ." Jeff Heath, New York, New York

40. What to Bring to an Interview

"Some candidates have what I call a 'brag book' . . ." Ron Reeves, Elgin, Illinois

"Your notepad should already include prepared questions for you to ask . . ." Cindy Lyness, Cedar Rapids, Iowa

41. Know How You Can Benefit the Company

"At MRI, we tell job candidates to think of FAB—Features, Accomplishments, and Benefits." Karen Egan, Grass Valley, California

42. Rehearse!

"Don't think you can 'wing it' during the interview." Cindy Lyness, Cedar Rapids, Iowa

44. Does Your Family Support You?

"It's essential to get your children, your spouse . . ." Mark Rosenthal, Atlanta, Georgia

". . . you have to consider your spouse's career . . ." Mark Rosenthal, Atlanta, Georgia

"You must communicate with your partner, . . ." Mark Rosenthal, Atlanta, Georgia

45. Landing a Job Is a Full-Time Job

". . . approach your search . . . as you would a job you love." Cindy Lyness, Cedar Rapids, Iowa

"Here at your home office . . ." Cindy Lyness, Cedar Rapids, Iowa

46. Last-Minute Preparations

"It's your chance to ask an all-important question: 'What's tomorrow's agenda?'" Robert Bassman, Plano, Texas

"If possible, make a dry run." Art Katz, Atlanta, Georgia

55. A Two-Way Conversation

". . . the better you do your homework, the more at ease you'll be. Preparation not only builds confidence, it relaxes you." Karen Bloomfield, Cleveland, Ohio

61. Be Focused

"One of my favorite movie scenes . . ." Bob Mannarino, Philadelphia, Pennsylvania

62. Lighten Up!

". . . don't feel as if your life depends on how you answer every question." Jim Cargill, Lake Tahoe, California

"One way to relieve anxiety is to arrive a few minutes early." Art Katz, Atlanta, Georgia

64. The Right Chemistry

"Make a positive comment about the geography." Gerry Kotler, Dayton, Ohio

"Say good things about the company." Gerry Kotler, Dayton, Ohio

"Praise the company's product or service." Gerry Kotler, Dayton, Ohio

66. Know When to Shut Up

". . . for fear that they may disclose confidential information." Jeff Heath, New York, New York

67. The Proactive Interview

"Let me see if I can make things clearer . . ." Jeff Heath, New York, New York

68. Opinion-Based Verses Behavior-Based Interviewing

"Our records indicate that under 50 percent of opinion-based inerviews . . ." Jim Dykeman, Mercer Island, Washington

"Behavioral-based interviewing also addresses a specific situation . . ." Jeff Kaye, Plano, Texas

"Prior to the interview, find out the hiring authority's agenda." Bob Bassman, Plano, Texas

69. Paint a Vivid Picture

"Be prepared to tell ministories of quantifiable accomplishments." James Dykeman, Mercer Island, Washington

"Candidates who articulate precisely what they do . . ." John Rosica, San Jose, California

"This is the problem I faced." Art Katz, Atlanta, Georgia

"By painting a vivid picture of what you have done . . ." Sam Sarafa, Ann Arbor, Michigan

70. Tell Them How Good You Are

"Suppose the President of the United States walked into my office . . ." Gerry Kotler, Dayton, Ohio

74. Be a Good Listener

"What would you like me to accomplish short term and long term in this position?" David Baranski, Chicago, Illinois

75. The Importance of Taking Good Notes

"It's a sign of respect for the interviewer's time," John Littman, Philadelphia, Pennsylvania

"When you prepare a thank-you note afterwards, . . ." PJ Jones, Pittsburgh, Pennsylvania

"It's lethal not to have questions," Harvey Bass, Sparta, New Jersey

"It makes you look conscientious," Ruth and Lance Incitta, Sparta, New Jersey

76. 15 Questions You Should Be Prepared to Answer

"How do you normally react to praise (criticism)?" Sandy and David Sanders, Roseville, California

"What was the worst decision you ever made?" How did you feel about it?" Sandy and David Sanders

79. Turn a Minus into a Plus

"I hate to lose." Steve Braun, Baltimore, Maryland

"Consider a salesperson who . . . is the only candidate without management experience . . ." Carolina Mapes, Omaha, Nebraska

"If something on your résumé or in your past stands out as a big minus, . . ." Rick Springer, Cleveland, Ohio

"Top executives understand that the only people who don't make mistakes . . ." Todd Provost, Dana Point, California

80. Be Open to New Ideas

"Comments such as, 'I'm a professional,' . . ." Jeff Heath, New York, New York

"You must give behavior-based explanations of how you initiated change . . ." Cy Tessin, Kalamazoo, Michigan

83. Avoid Confrontation

"Some interviewers will purposely provoke you to see how react . . ." Russ Hanson, Appleton, Wisconsin

87. Fire in the Belly

"One of my clients actually conducts a 'FITB test.'" Chris Walhof, Boise, Idaho

88. Building Rapport

"She had all the qualifications we were looking for . . ." David Baranski, Chicago, Illinois

"Today's companies are looking for candidates who know how to actively listen . . ." Stacy Gulden, Winter Park, Florida

"Showing a genuine interest in the company is also an effective way to build rapport." Jeff Heath, New York, New York

93. Give Sincere Compliments

"I am very pleased to meet you . . . I am happy to be here." Art Katz, Atlanta, Georgia

94. Multiple Interviews

"Prepare for every interview as if it were your first." David Baranski, Chicago, Illinois

"Each person has a different agenda and different expectations of you." Bob Bassman, Plano, Texas

"It's possible that during the course of several interviews, one interviewer will be the designated 'bad guy.'" Russ Hanson, Appleton, Wisconsin

95. The Panel Interview

"Trying to guess who's the most important in the room . . ." David Baranski, Chicago, Illinois

96. Doing Lunch

"There's a story that Thomas Edison wouldn't hire someone who salted his food without first tasting it." Feather Tippetts, San Jose, California

99. Be Flexible

"If jobs were perfect, there would be no search firms." David Baranski, Chicago, Illinois

101. Closing the Interview

"I feel comfortable with you and with the position we've discussed." David Baranski, Chicago, Illinois

"Do you have any concerns about my ability to do the job and fit in?" David Baranski, Chicago, Illinois

"I feel comfortable with you and the position we discussed." David Baranski, Chicago, Illinois

"How do I compare to the other candidates you have interviewed?" David Baranski

"I have a lot of information and everything I need . . ." James Dykeman, Mercer Island, Washington

"What's the next step?" James Dykeman, Mercer Island, Washington

"When should I follow up with you?" Jeff Kaye, Plano, Texas

"Is there anything personally or professionally that you believe would . . ." Jeff Kaye

"I am very impressed with what I've seen here." Gerry Kotler, Dayton, Ohio

"Mr. Employer, your search is over." Art Sheehan, Del Ray Beach, Florida

102. Creating a Sense of Urgency

"I have other offers pending . . ." Gerry Kotler, Dayton, Ohio

"Is there anything that I have said that indicated I'm not perfect for the job?" Harvey Bass, Sparta, New Jersey

"My family is scheduled to make a move within a couple of weeks." James Weber, Coral Gables, Florida

103. Don't Keep It a Secret

"I really want this job." Mary and Michael Mayher, Raleigh, North Carolina

105. Playing Hard to Get

"You have my attention and I like what you put on the table." James Dykeman, Mercer Island, Washington

106. Money Talk

"What I am being paid now is for a different job and a different company." Steve Kendall, Atlanta, Georgia

"A hiring authority may also ask, 'How much will it take for you to accept this position?'" Sam Sarafa, Ann Arbor, Michigan

108. How to Use Your Headhunter *after* the Interview

"Immediately following each interview, the first person you should contact is your headhunter," Jeffrey Heath, New York, New York

"If you don't get an offer, he'll have the scoop," Cindy Lyness, Cedar Rapids, Iowa

110. More Money Talk

"Make it known you're not strictly driven by money," Sam Sarafa, Ann Arbor, Michigan

"If it's not too low, you have a place to start negotiating," Jeff Kaye, Plano, Texas

112. Nonsalary Remuneration

". . .the whole package can be worth a lot more . . ." Kimberly Barden, Grass Valley, California

"If you like everything else about the job, . . ." Jeff Kaye, Plano, Texas

113. Sleep on It

"Make your decision quickly—preferably before your head hits the pillow that night!" Ron Whitney, Sacramento, California

"There's always the risk that while you sleep on it, . . ." Steve Kendall, Atlanta, Georgia

117. Coaching Your References

"I think XYZ Company has a lot of opportunity." PJ Jones, Pittsburgh, Pennsylvania

"A satisfied customer is among the best references," Sandy and David Sanders, Roseville, California

"If your former company has a policy against giving references," Cindy Lyness, Cedar Rapids, Iowa

"Ask your references to be open and honest." Peter Isenberg, Noblesville, Indiana

"Include a third-party business reference." Ron Whitney, Sacramento, California

119. Restrictive Covenants

A special acknowledgment to Don Goldman, MRI general counsel, for sharing his expertise on this subject of restrictive covenants.

120. Review Your Plan Documents and Contracts

Don Goldman, MRI general counsel, is the source for advice on reviewing plan documents.

Index

About the Authors

Alan R. Schonberg is chairman and founder of Management Recruiters International (MRI), the world's largest search and recruitment organization, with 5000 headhunters in 1000 offices around the world. Each year, MRI helps organizations find and hire over 30,000 middle and senior managers.

Robert L. Shook is the author of over 40 books, including *The Greatest Sales Stories Ever Told, I'll Get Back to You,* and *The IBM Way.*